The Hand of God In American History

Three Books in One

Edited By

Michael D. Fortner

Great Plains Press, Lawton, OK

Edition 1.1, 2013
Copyright © 2013 by Great Plains Press All rights reserved

No part of this book may be reproduced, stored in a retrieval system, or transmitted in any form or by any means, electronic, mechanical, recording or otherwise, without written permission by the copyright holder.

All underlining within quoted material and Scripture is by the author unless otherwise stated.

Library of Congress Catalog-in-Publication Data: 2013930119

Author: Fortner, Michael
Title: The Hand of God in American History

1. U.S. History 2. Christian History 3. Christianity 4. Divine Providence

Three Books in One
Contains

Book One 5
THE HAND OF GOD IN AMERICAN HISTORY
A Study of Divine Providence as Seen in the Life and Mission of a Nation

By: Wilbur Fisk Tillett, D.D.,LL.D.

Professor of Christian Doctrine in the School of Religion, and Dean Emeritus of the Theological Faculty in Vanderbilt University

Cokesbury Press, Nashville, TN
Copyright 1923, LAMAR & BARTON

****

Book Two 40
THE HAND OF GOD IN AMERICAN HISTORY

A Discourse Delivered in the Baptist Church, Keeseville, NY
July 7, 1861

By: John F. Bigelow
Pastor of Keeseville Baptist Church

Also
Before The United Literary Societies of New Hampton Institution,
Fairfax, VT, July 15, 1861

****

Book Three 75

GOD'S HAND IN AMERICA

By: The Rev. George B. Cheever
With an Essay, by The Rev. Dr. skinner

New York: M. W. Dodd, Brick Church Chapel
Originally published 1841

A Note From the Publisher

In my research of American History I found five books that were all published with a similar title about God's hand in American history. I have here reproduced the best three of those books. They are different enough that they compliment each other rather than repeat.

I have updated the spelling of some words, such as "to-day" to "today." And I have put the meaning of some very archaic words in brackets [ ], but there are still some old words and old spellings. Occasionally I put [sic] to let the reader know that the word before it is in fact spelled the way it was in the original book. I also shortened a number of very long paragraphs.

You will notice that in this book there are no "end notes" at the end of the chapter or the end of the book. The reason there are no end notes is because it is very troublesome for a reader to lookup the note which may have some important information that will go unread or may only be "Ibid." It is especially difficult to have end notes with an eBook, therefore, this book has been formatted exactly as its eBook version, with notes in the text.

The Amazon Kindle edition of this book is available for only $.99 cents. You don't need to own a Kindle reader, you can download the book and read it on your PC with the free Kindle for PC program available at amazon.com.

Michael D. Fortner, Editor, Publisher

Book One

THE HAND OF GOD IN AMERICAN HISTORY
A Study of Divine Providence as Seen in the Life and Mission of a Nation

By: Wilbur Fisk Tillett, D.D.,LL.D.

Professor of Christian Doctrine in the School of Religion, and Dean Emeritus of the Theological Faculty in Vanderbilt University

Cokesbury Press, Nashville, TN
Copyright 1923, LAMAR & BARTON

"The last and noblest effort of Divine Providence in behalf of the human race" is what Ralph Waldo Emerson calls the United States of America. The word "America" has come to be used throughout the world as a designation of this one large and influential republic of the North American Continent; and if we so use it, it is simply in compliance with accepted usage and widespread custom, and not because we fail to recognize the importance and greatness of other countries and nations in North and South America.

Table of Contents

Chapter 1: God's Use of Nations 6
Chapter 2: Christopher Columbus, The Christ-Bearer 8
Chapter 3: The Faith of Our Fathers 10
Chapter 4: The Religious Faith and Moral Character of Our Presidents 16
Chapter 5: Our Ethical Idealism and Altruism 26
Chapter 6: What Makes a Nation Great? 36

Chapter 1
GOD'S USE OF NATIONS

If God does his work in this world through men, as indeed he ever does, he needs men collectively as well as individually for the accomplishment of his purposes. If human governments and nations are, as indeed they are, a necessity in the world, they are a necessity to God as well as to men. Has anything short of Divine Omnipotence such power for good as a holy nation whose government is founded upon the principles of righteousness, and which is con ducted so as to promote intelligence and righteousness among its own people and throughout the earth? To answer these questions, as they must be answered, affirmatively, means that nations no less than individuals, even more than individuals, are instruments of Divine Providence, Never before in the history of the world have the power and influence of nations, alike for evil and for good, been so manifest as they are today; and never before has there been a time more fitting than the present, for the profitable study of the providential mission of a nation. If men will do, when collectively organized into corporations and governments, what they will not do as individuals, and this we know to be true, it is of the highest importance that along with national consciousness there should be developed a national conscience.

In studying God's providential government of nations and his relations to civil governments, we must never lose sight of the fact that governments and nations are not impersonal things and passive puppets in the Hand of Omnipotence, but free human beings collected in groups and organized in masses, and that God's providential government of them is subject to all the conditions and limitations involved in his government of individuals as free beings.

Among the eminent philosophers of the world who have believed in Divine Providence, none was more pronounced and outspoken in expressing his convictions than Hegel. He regarded *"history as a spacious book of Providence recording how the deeds of men and nations have helped or hindered the purposes of God."* He believed that the providence of God was exercised on a *"large and grand scale,"* and protested against that "peddling view of Providence 11 which sees the Hand of God in the comparatively unimportant and trifling details of individual life, but not in the large and great affairs of nations and of the universe. His *"Philosophy of History"* is one long protest against the position, on the one hand, of those who limit the guiding Hand of God to the life and needs of individuals (for example, when help has unexpectedly come to an individual in great perplexity), and on the other hand, of those who believe in Divine Providence only in general, but not in the particulars and details that are involved in the processes of life alike of individuals and of nations. When the lives of individuals and the histories of nations are thus viewed, they become not only a record of human annals, but a study of Divine Providence in things both small and great.

We desire to point out some providential facts and circumstances in the history of America, drawn, not to any considerable extent from its religious and ecclesiastical history, but mainly from its civic life and what it is common to call secular history, finding perchance something sacred in the secular and much that is divine in what is most human.

Chapter 2
Christopher Columbus The Christ-Bearer

Among the many facts and circumstances that prove that this nation had its inspiration and origin in the hearts and consciences of those who believed in Divine Providence and in Christ as the rightful Ruler of men and nations, we call attention first to its discovery in 1492.

Christopher Columbus regarded himself as engaged in a distinctly Christian mission, when, after committing himself and his company in prayer to the guidance of God, he went forth to discover whatever unknown worlds might lie between Spain and the East Indies. "Christopher," his baptismal name, means the *"Christ-bearer,"* and he ever regarded himself as being, by his very christening, *"the called of God."* He regarded his voyage of discovery as a kind of missionary journey. *"God made me,"* he says, *"a messenger of the new heavens and the new earth."* And when this New World was discovered, he lost no time in claiming it for Christ. Erecting a cross on landing, he christened the new world *"San Salvador"* (St. Saviour), joined with his companions in singing the *"Gloria in Excelsis,"* and began at once pro claiming Christ to the new and strange people whom he found here. The discovery of America was indeed a reward of faith.

Joaquin Miller, the American poet, although approaching and interpreting the mind and mission of Columbus from a different angle, makes him thereby no less an instrument of Divine Providence than do they who call attention to the religious faith and motives that characterized him. Miller's poem titled "Columbus" is in every way worthy of his theme, and of quotation in this study of the providential events and lessons in American history:

Behind him lay the gray Azores,
Behind the gates of Hercules;

Before him not the ghost of shores,
Before him only shoreless seas.
The good mate said: "Now must we pray,
For lo! the very stars are gone.
Brave Admiral, speak, what shall I say?"
"Why, say; 'Sail on! sail on! and on!'"

"My men grow mutinous, day by day,
My men grow ghastly wan and weak."
The stout mate thought of home; a spray
Of salt wave washed his swarthy cheek.
"What shall I say, brave Admiral, say,
If we sight naught but seas at dawn?"
"Why, you shall say at break of day,
'Sail on! sail on! sail on! and on!'"

They sailed and sailed, as winds might blow,
Until at last the blanched mate said:
"Why, now not even God would know.
Should I and all my men fall dead;
These very winds forget their way,
For God from these dread seas is gone.
Now speak, brave Admiral, speak and say"—
He said: "Sail on! sail on! and on!"

They sailed. They sailed. Then spake the mate:
"This mad sea shows his teeth tonight;
He curls his lip, he lies in wait,
With lifted teeth, as if to bite!
Brave Admiral, say but one good word:
What shall we do when hope is gone?"
"The words leapt like a leaping sword:
"Sail on! sail on! sail on! and on!"

Then, pale and worn, he kept his deck,
And peered through darkness. Ah, that night
Of all dark nights! And then a speck—
A light! a light! a light! a light!
It grew, a starlit flag unfurled!
It grew to be Time's burst of dawn.
He gained a world; he gave that world
Its grandest lesson: "On! sail on!" *

(* Copyrighted by Whitaker & Ray-Wiggin Company. Printed by permission.)

Chapter 3
The Faith Of Our Fathers

We think that facts can be adduced to prove that no great nation in the history of the world has ever been founded under conditions and influences so distinctly moral and religious, and by persons so thoroughly Christian in their ideals, motives, and aims, as we may with confidence claim is true of America. Bishop Galloway has truly said, in his volume entitled *"Christianity and the American Commonwealth"*:

> The deepest and mightiest thing in any nation's heart is its religion; therefore as is the religion, so is the nation. I hesitate not to affirm that the temple at Jerusalem was built by a no more sacred patriotism or under the benedictions of a no more favoring Providence than were the colonial governments of this new world. Christian teachings were the seed thoughts of our political constitutions. If we eliminate from our national history the influence of the Christian religion, we have nothing left but a set of disjointed facts without moral significance.

The years that intervened between the departure of Columbus from these shores and the Declaration of Independence in 1776 were years of providential preparation in which were laid, in the peoples that came hither, and in the ideals and motives that actuated them, the foundations of a nation that may be justified in claiming to be an *"elect nation of God"* if it shall prove itself such by service to God and man.

The people who settled in this country in the first instance were the picked Christian men and women of the civilized world. They constituted the sturdy stuff out of which the noblest type of Christian citizenship and the most heroic type of Christian manhood and womanhood are made. Many motives prompted the coming of the colonists to this country, but it can easily be shown that the greatest of them all was religion, the desire for religious and civil freedom to make possible the highest development of moral character and personality in themselves and their children.

In the first settlement made by the English in North America in 1606 (that in Virginia) the charter of the new colony gave special emphasis to the large place which the Christian religion was to have in the life of the new colony. The charter declared of the colony at Jamestown that it was designed that *"under the providence of God it might tend to the glory of his Divine Majesty in propagating the Christian religion to such people as yet live in darkness and miserable ignorance of the true knowledge and worship of God.* The first building erected by the young colony in Virginia was a house for Christian worship. The *"Mayflower Compact"* of 1620 declared that, foremost among the objects that brought the "Pilgrim Fathers*'" to this country was *"the glory of God and the advancement of Christian faith."* The *"Articles of Confederation of the New England Colonies,"* 1643, begin with these words: *"Whereas we all came into these parts of America with one and the same end and aim, namely, to advance the kingdom of our Lord Jesus Christ, and to enjoy the liberties of the gospel in purity and peace; and whereas in our settling, by a wise providence of God, we are further dispersed upon the seacoasts and rivers than we at first intended, etc."*— words which show their recognition of and dependence upon the guiding Hand of God.

The Huguenots who came to this country were the very flower of the Christian manhood and womanhood of France. Driven by persecution from their native land, they found a welcome home in the Carolinas and elsewhere in America. A country never welcomed a finer type of Christian character and heroism to its shores than that of the French Huguenot. In the face of both royal and ecclesiastical despot ism, they dared to contend for freedom of con science, freedom of worship, and freedom of speech, the three essential principles of all religious and civic liberty; and not being allowed to hold such sentiments in France, they turned to the one and only land that gave such sentiments and those who held them a hospitable welcome. Henry Cabot Lodge says that in proportion to their numbers the Huguenots have produced and given to the American republic more men of character and ability than any other class of early settlers in this country.

"*The State of Georgia was colonized expressly as an asylum for imprisoned and persecuted Protestants.*" So writes Dr. Baird, the Church historian. "*No colony of all the thirteen had a more distinctly Christian origin than this. Godly Moravians from Germany, devout Church men and pious Puritans from England, brave Highlanders from Scotland, the heroic Salzburgers from the Alps—all found a cordial welcome here.*" The history of these Salzburger colonists Bishop Hurst refers to as "*one of the most remarkable records of a patient, pure, and uncomplaining religious body in the whole history of the Christian Church.*"

The Scotch-Irish who settled in the upper valleys of Virginia and in the Piedmont sections of Virginia and North Carolina were the very embodiment of sturdy and conscientious Christian manhood. In the fiber of their moral character they were made of granite, of flint, of iron. They stand today, and have always stood, for all that is best in our Christian civilization.

The Dutch who settled in New York were not so distinctly and avowedly religious as the other early settlers in the motives that led them to come to this country; but their dominant motives were moral and civic, and not commercial, and they had back of them a history full of moral heroism, as shown in the long struggle for civil and religious liberty that made them just such a type of sturdy, solid Christian manhood as was needed in the New World to lay the foundation for what has since become the metropolis of the nation. These Dutch settlers take pride in claiming to have built "*the first free church and the first free school in America.*"

Even the Roman Catholic colony, which was established by Lord Baltimore in what became the State of Maryland, became the most liberal and progressive type of Roman Catholicism which the world has ever seen. Their charter, obtained from the Protestant King of England, guaranteed perfect religious liberty, an almost unheard-of thing for Roman Catholicism to do in that day.

The contrast in character between these early settlers, between these heroic and high-minded men and women who came to these shores and created our republic, and the human riffraff that is now drifting into this "*melting pot*" of the Western world is painful to contemplate, and calls for the most serious consideration and the wisest possible legislation, lest we as a nation in discharging our duty to others find that instead of our lifting these immigrant hordes up, we allow them to pull the nation down with their low, Godless, un-American ideals and social vices.

However desirable Christian unity may be and however objectionable and hurtful a needless multiplication of religious denominations may be, we count it a fortunate thing that there were many different and independent types of Christian experience, character, and faith that met together here in those early days. This tended to make the resultant type of Christian civilization and government that was developed in this country singularly free from bigotry and sectarian narrowness, and more genuinely liberal than could have been the case had all been of one type of religious faith. The fact that there are and have always been in this country many different religious denominations is not a thing to be deplored as wholly evil. The different Churches have influenced each other for good, and have tended to make each other broad and charitable, and have thus helped to create and maintain that ideal of civil and religious liberty which is the crown and glory of our republic. The growth of Christianity in this country and the contribution of American Christianity to world evangelization—neither of which has ever before been equaled in any country in any period of history—are in no small degree a resultant of the facts and conditions here referred to and are, as much as anything can be, a proof of the Hand of God in our history. But of this phase of our providential history we are not here writing in detail.

The Declaration of Independence, 1776, recognized in unmistakable terms the Divine Being and the need of the new-born nation for his blessing as they claimed for themselves the in alienable rights which they were entitled to *"under the laws of Nature and Nature's God,"* such rights as all men had been *"endowed with by their Creator."* It was *"with a firm reliance on the protection of Divine Providence"* that they *"pledged to each other their lives, their fortunes, and their sacred honor."* In the *"Articles of Confederation,"* drawn up a year later, reference is made to how *"it hath pleased the Great Governor of the world to incline the hearts of the Legislatures to the articles of con federation and perpetual union."* At a time like this there was but one step between what might turn out to be the highest patriotism, in one event, and the crime of treason, if it ended otherwise. *"There is but one step between me and death,"* said a young man once who became later Israel's greatest king. One of these revolutionary patriots facetiously said: *"Unless we all hang together, we are sure to hang separately."* But the sequel proved that God's hand was at the helm, and that some political revolutions are providential.

The Colonial Congress, which was the highest governing body in this country from the Declaration of Independence in 1776 to the inauguration of George Washington as President in 1789, recognized repeatedly, in public utterances addressed to the people, *"the government of Almighty God," "the merits and mediation of Jesus Christ,"* and the value of the Christian religion as the best means *"for the promotion and enlargement of that kingdom which consisteth in righteousness, peace, and joy in the Holy Ghost."* This Congress (in 1782) passed a resolution that recognized the sanctity of the Holy Scriptures and their great value to the nation.

At this historic Federal Convention which met in 1787 to make a Constitution for the new government of the United States, George Washing ton being in the chair, the venerable Benjamin Franklin made a motion that the exercises of the Convention be opened daily with prayer, declaring as he did so, in the following words, his faith in an overruling Providence:

> I have lived, sir, a long time, and the longer I live the more convincing proofs I see that God governs in the affairs of men. And if a sparrow cannot fall to the ground without his notice, is it possible that an empire can rise without his aid? We have been assured, sir, in the sacred writings, that, "except the Lord build the house, they labor in vain that build it." I firmly believe this, and I also believe that without his concurring aid we shall succeed, in this political building, no better than the builders of Babel.

"I have never doubted the existence of the Deity," said this truly typical American citizen and statesman on another occasion; *"nor have I ever doubted that He made the world and governs it by his Providence; that the most acceptable service of God is doing good to man; that our souls are immortal; and that all crime will be punished and virtue rewarded either here or hereafter."*

If a man like Benjamin Franklin could feel and talk thus, we may be sure that there was a multitude of believers in God's Providence in that critical and constructive period in the life of the young Republic who in faith and prayer committed to the Hand Divine the ship of state which they were launching on the perilous sea of history.

While ethical ideals and spiritual forces have most to do with the making of a great nation, and with its fulfillment of a great mission, it is also true that national greatness is not independent of natural and physical conditions. Spiritual treasures are in earthen vessels, and a people, in order to be great and do great things, must have a land to live in and cultivate which is favorable to their highest and best development. And so we find that Robert Ellis Thompson in writing of the Hand of God in American history calls attention to the rare combination of physical features and conditions that are found in the United States, and declares them to be a part and a proof of the Divine Providence that has designed and prepared America for a providential mission in the earth:

> The natural resources of our three millions of square miles are such as to constitute this the most valuable division of the earth's surface possessed by any people It contains more land capable of human cultivation, more navigable waters in its lakes and rivers, more extensive mineral deposits, and larger pastures, than does any other national area. . . . Providence seems to have kept the most valuable thing in the New World from notice, until the fit people was ready to occupy this region which now exceeds all the rest of the continent in the numbers of its population, its accumulations of wealth, its diffusion of intelligence, and its high standard of living.

Chapter 4
The Religious Faith And Moral Character Of Our Presidents

If nations are instruments of Divine Providence, the faith and character of rulers is a matter of vital moment. Under a free democratic system of government, where the people choose from among themselves periodically their own rulers, the moral ideals of the people find expression in the type and character of the men chosen as rulers; and these leaders and representatives of the people, therefore, are in turn, in a sense, an expression of the moral character of the people whose public servants they are. This at least is here true in democracies to an extent that cannot be true where thrones are inherited and rulers are born rather than selected by the people in view of their qualities and fitness for leadership. If *"like people like priest"* was said of Israel, *"like people like president"* may be said of the American democracy.

An examination and study of the representative rulers and chief magistrates of the American people will reveal the fact that the men selected to fill the office of President, taken as a whole, embody, in no small degree, in their private life and personal character, and also in their public and official acts, the ethical ideals of the Christian religion. No debauchery and basely immoral use of office such as has often made infamous the annals of the royal families of the world in the past has ever blackened the history of our Presidential office. We can select only a few for special study—and our highest and greatest these will be, but in moral character and fidelity to duty no better than others. If a Divine Hand guides a nation, it must be upon the rulers who determine and shape its policies.

George Washington, our first President, was a devout and consistent member of the Protestant Episcopal Church. In his first official utterance as President appears the following declaration of his faith in an overruling Providence:

> It would be peculiarly improper to omit, in this first official act, my fervent supplication to that Almighty Being who rules over the universe, who presides in the councils of nations, and whose providential aid can supply every human defect that his benediction may consecrate to the liberties and happiness of the people of the United States, a government instituted by themselves for these essential purposes, and may enable every instrument employed in its administration to execute with success the functions allotted to his charge. In tendering this homage to the great Author of every public and private good, I assure myself that it expresses your sentiments not less than my own, and those of our fellow-citizens at large not less than our own. No people can be bound to acknowledge and adore the invisible Hand which conducts the affairs of men more than the people of the United States. Every step by which they have advanced to the character of an independent nation seems to have been distinguished by some token of providential agency.

After eight years at the head of our national government Washington retired, and in doing so delivered a farewell address that has been pronounced one of the most masterful State papers ever written by any ruler. It contains words no less significant of the estimate which he placed upon religion than the above words uttered at the beginning of his presidency:

> Of all the dispositions and habits which lead to political prosperity, religion and morality are indispensable supports. In vain would that man claim the tribute of patriotism who should labor to subvert these great pillars of human happiness, these firmest props of the duties of men and citizens. The mere politician, equally with the pious man, ought to respect and cherish them. A volume could not trace all their connections with private and public felicity. Let it simply be asked: Where is the security for property, for reputation, for life, if the sense of religious obligation desert the oaths which are the instruments of investigation in courts of justice? And let us with caution indulge the supposition that morality can be maintained without religion. Whatever may be conceded to the influence of refined education on minds of peculiar structure, reason and experience both forbid us to expect that national morality can prevail in exclusion of religious principle.

These are golden words. Could a Christian nation ask from its first, most honored, and most representative ruler a better declaration than this of faith in Divine Providence and in religion as the foundation of national morality and greatness?

"*In fortitude, justice, and equanimity,*" says Walter Savage Landor, "*no man ever excelled George Washington. No exemplar has been recommended to our gratitude, love, and veneration, by the most impartial historian, or the most encomiastic biographer, in whom so many and so great virtues, public and private, were united.*"

Thomas Jefferson is frequently referred to as a. skeptic in religious opinions. But a recent writer, in an introduction to a late reprint of what is known as "*the Thomas Jefferson Bible,*" says concerning him that this impression is altogether erroneous. This "*Jefferson Bible*" is the best possible proof that could be given of Jefferson's profound reverence for Christ, He titled it "*The life and morals of Jesus of Nazareth extracted textually from the Gospels of Matthew, Mark, Luke, and John.*" He prepared it in French, Greek, and Latin as well as in English. This same writer says of him:

> Thomas Jefferson was from early life a close student of the Bible. It was of the Bible that he wrote: "*There never was a more pure or sublime system of morality than is to be found in the four evangelists.*" His further interest in it is clearly shown by the original copy of the so-called "*Jefferson, Bible,*" now pre served with so much care in the National Museum at Washing ton, it having been purchased by the United States government as a memento of the author of the Declaration of Independence, and is now a priceless relic of that great man. It is a little leather-bound volume resembling in appearance an old account book, and on its pages may be read the life of Christ, prepared by arranging chronologically all of the verses from the four Gospels that pertain to the career of our Lord, omitting, however, "*every verse or paragraph that to his mind was ambiguous or controversial, and every statement of fact that would not have been admitted as evidence in a court of justice.*" . . .
>
> Jefferson was an indefatigably zealous student of the Bible, and was infinitely more conversant with it than the bulk of professed Christians. The framing of the Declaration of Independence reveals a strongly religious mind. His religious belief has been questioned, and yet he was a member of the Episcopal Church in Charlottesville, Va., contributing regularly to its support and serving as a member of its vestry. He wrote of himself: "*I am a Christian in the only sense Christ wished any one to be—sincerely attached to his doctrines in preference to all others.*"

Jefferson expressed the wish toward the close of his life that he might be remembered by posterity simply as *"the author of the Declaration of Independence, of the statute in Virginia for religious freedom, and the Father of the. University of Virginia."*

While Abraham Lincoln was not a member of any Church, those who knew him best in later life declare confidently that he was a true Christian, He took occasion often to declare his faith in the overruling providence of Almighty God and in the efficacy of prayer. He' said once to an intimate friend: *"When any Church shall inscribe over its altars as its sole qualification for membership the Saviour's condensed statement of the substance of both law and gospel, 'Thou shalt love the Lord thy God with all thy heart, and with all thy mind, and thy neighbor as thyself,' that Church will I join with all my heart and all my soul."* In the Lincoln Museum at Washington is an old Bible whose well-thumbed pages show that it was much used by the owner. The owner's name is plainly written on the inside of the cover: *"A. Lincoln, his own book."*

He was all through his life a devout student of this Book, and from it he made more quotations in his conversation and in his speeches than from any and all other sources. He came into the presidential office under the most trying conditions that ever confronted any President, and the profound sense of responsibility which he was under and which almost overwhelmed him at times drove him to realize the need of God's help and guidance and made him a man of faith and prayer. When on his way to Washington City to be inaugurated, he uttered the following impressive words:

> I go to assume a task more difficult than that which has devolved upon any other man since the days of Washington. He never would have succeeded but for the aid of Divine Providence, upon which he at all times relied. I feel that I cannot succeed without the same divine blessing which sustained him, and on the same Almighty Being I place my reliance for support. And I hope you, my friends, will all pray that I may receive the divine assistance without which I cannot succeed, but with which success is certain.

A confident and zealous clergyman once re marked to Mr. Lincoln during the war: *"I am sure we are going to win, because we have God on our side."* *"My friend,"* Mr. Lincoln replied, *"what I want to be sure of is, that we are on God's side. That is the all-important thing for us to know."* They who fought for *"States'*

Rights" and "*State Sovereignty*" may have contended for a legitimate principle of government and a worthy cause; but whosoever, in any land at any time, fights for the perpetuation of human slavery, is fighting against the sun and the stars of heaven and against the sure Providence of God. No section of the United States is more devoutly thankful than the South is today that God in his Providence brought slavery to an end and preserved the Union intact.

The whole nation, however, and not the South alone, was responsible for the institution of slavery. In the earlier days of the Republic it existed in New England and elsewhere in the North, and when the slave owners there, after due experiment, found slavery unprofitable because of rigorous climatic conditions and growing antipathy to the institution, they sold their slaves to cotton planters of the South, and the sentiment against slavery thereafter rapidly developed throughout all the nonslaveholding States. Even Peter Faneuil, the founder of the "*Cradle of Liberty*" after whom the historic "*Faneuil Hall*" of Boston, famous for its anti-slavery meetings and pronouncements, was named, was at one time a slave-trader. In the meantime it can be said—though it is no justification of the institution of slavery to say it— that among all the millions of negroes in the world those who live in America today, taken as a whole, enjoy more of the comforts and blessings and privileges of life than those found in any other land. If the North as well as the South is responsible for this blemish upon our history, it is also true that the people of the South today no less than those of the North count it providential that slavery was long ago brought to an end and rejoice in the Providence that removed this moral incubus and obstacle to progress from the body politic of our nation.

No greater misfortune ever happened to the South, in connection with the Civil War, than the death of Abraham Lincoln at the time and under the conditions in which he died. Many things that followed the war in the South would have been less odious and grievous to the Southern people if he had lived. It is doubtless true that the successful termination of the war for the abolition of slavery and his tragic death at the end of it had the inevitable effect of making him, in the eyes both of the American nation and of the whole world, an even greater hero than he would have been adjudged to be, had he lived and served the country in a period of peace. While this is true, it is also true that it was a long time before the people of the South, especially the older generation that took part in the Civil War, could do justice to Lincoln and appreciate him for his real and true worth. But there are few Southerners left today who can read without sympathetic emotion and profound appreciation the tribute which was paid to him at his death by Walt Whitman in the finest poem he ever wrote:

> O Captain! my Captain! our fearful trip is done;
> The ship has weathered every rack, the prize we sought is won;
> The port is near, the bells I hear, the people all exulting,
> While follow eyes the steady keel, the vessel grim and daring:
> But O heart! heart! heart!
> O the bleeding drops of red,
> Where on the deck my Captain lies,
> Fallen, cold, and dead!
> O Captain! my Captain! rise up and hear the bells!
> Rise up! for you the flag is flung, for you the bugle trills,
> For you bouquets and ribboned wreaths, for you the shores a-crowding,
> For you they call, the swaying mass, their eager faces turning:
> Here, Captain! dear father,
> This arm beneath your head!
> It is some dream that on the deck
> You've fallen cold and dead!
>
> My Captain does not answer, his lips are pale and still;
> My father does not feel my arm, he has no pulse, no will:
> The ship is anchored safe and sound, its voyage closed and done;
> From fearful trip the victor ship comes in with object won! Exult, O shores, and ring, O bells!
> But I with mournful tread, Walk the deck my Captain lies, Fallen, cold, and dead.

(Copyrighted by Small, Maynard & Co. Printed by permission.)

Let us hope that the Providence that turned the selling of Joseph into slavery and the four centuries of Hebrew bondage in Egypt into ultimate good for the whole world as well as for the slaves themselves, even though it was meant by men for evil, will in some way overrule the apprenticeship in slavery which some of the negro race have served in this country to the ultimate intellectual, moral, and social good of their entire race, not only here, but in darkest Africa and elsewhere throughout the world.

A Southern Confederate soldier-poet, writing of the battle of Gettysburg, speaks for others as well as himself when he sees the Hand of God in the final issues of that bloody battle and of the civil war, and uses these true and beautiful words:

> They fell who lifted up a hand,
> And bade the sun in heaven to stand;
> They smote and fell, who set the bars
> Against the progress of the stars,
> And stayed the march of Mother-land,
>
> They stood who saw the future come
> On through the fight's delirium;
> They smote and stood, who held the hope
> Of nations on that slippery slope.
> Amid the cheers of Christendom.
>
> God lives! He forged the iron will
> Which grasped and held that trembling hill;
> God lives and reigns; he built and lent
> Those heights for Freedom's battlement,
> Where floats her flag in triumph still,
>
> Fold up the banners, smelt the guns!
> Love rules, her mightier purpose runs.
> The mighty Mother turns in tears
> The record of her battle years,
> Lamenting all her fallen sons.

(These lines were written by William H. Thompson, who fought as a private in a Georgia regiment, and himself took part in the battle concerning which he writes.)

Grover Cleveland, being the son of a Presbyterian clergyman, got his start in life where many other great men have been born and reared, in a preacher's home where economy and simplicity of life united with Christian culture and refinement to make conditions most favor able to starting an American youth upon a promising public career, And yet, in spite of the moral and religious atmosphere in which he was reared there was later at least one episode in his early mature life that was unsavory and to his discredit. Just after his nomination for the Presidential office, his political enemies did what politicians of all parties and all ages are given to doing—unearthed his past record and prepared at once to make large use of this discreditable incident in his earlier life, hoping thus to accomplish his defeat. His campaign managers upon learning of what was up were much disturbed, and fearing that the publication of the story would contribute to the defeat of their candidate unless it was denied, or offset in some manner, they telegraphed their leader asking his authority for denying it, or, if this should not be done, asking him to tell them what to say. The answer was telegraphed back at once, *"Tell them the truth. GROVER CLEVELAND."* His reply was so frank and quick, and his recognition that he must face and not shun his own past record, was so sincere and open, that this incident in the campaign resulted in winning rather than losing votes. It made the people feel that he would carry that same honesty and straightforwardness into his administration of the affairs of the nation; and in this they were not disappointed.

Both as a man and as President, he had "backbone" and the courage of his convictions. These sturdy qualities, if they led to his defeat in standing for re-election at the end of his first term, resulted four years later in causing the people to send him back to the White House for another term. But there is better proof than this of his being worthy to be selected by us as one of the five presidents whose strong moral qualities and acts have served both to create and to express our high American ideal of one who fills our Presidential office.

Among the State papers on file in the archives of our nation's history, there is perhaps none that could be more fittingly selected to set forth the high ethical ideal of the American people in matters of international ethics, than the message which President Grover Cleveland sent to Congress just after the forcible, and what he believed to be unwarranted, military occupation by United States soldiers of the Hawaiian Islands in 1893, which occupation Mr. Cleveland believed to be a breach of both national and international ethics. It was not a question, as he conceived it, to be settled by the political aspirations and desires and the commercial interests of the United States (both of which rendered desirable the annexation of the Islands), but it was rather, as he insisted, an occasion when a Christian nation should subordinate selfish interests to that standard of Christian ethics which ought to be the first and highest law for the regulation of a nation's dealings with another nation—and all the more so if this other nation be, as was the case in this instance, at the mercy of the larger and more powerful nation.

A few quotations from this document will suffice to justify our high estimate of it as an expression of the ethical ideals of the nation:

> I suppose that right and justice should determine the path to be followed in treating this subject. If national honesty is to be disregarded and a desire for territorial extension, or dissatisfaction with a form of government not our own, ought to regulate our conduct, I have entirely misapprehended the mission and character of our Government and the behavior which the con science of our people demands of their public servants. . . . The queen knew that she could not withstand the power of the United States, but she believed that she might safely trust to its justice. . . . It has been the boast of our Government that it seeks to do justice in all things without regard to the strength or weakness of those with whom it deals, I mistake the American people if they favor the odious doctrine that there is no such thing as international morality; that there is one law for a strong nation, and another for a weak one, and that even by indirection a strong power may with impunity despoil a weak one of its territory. . . . A substantial wrong has thus been done which a due regard for our national character as well as for the rights of the injured people requires that we should endeavor to repair. . . .
>
> The law of nations is founded upon reason and justice, and the rules of conduct governing individual relations between citizens or subjects of a civilized state are equally applicable as between enlightened nations. The consideration that international law is without a court for its enforcement and that obedience to its commands practically depends upon good faith instead of upon the mandate of a superior tribunal only gives additional sanction to the law itself, and brands any deliberate infraction of it not merely as a wrong but as a disgrace. A man of true honor protects the unwritten word which binds his conscience more scrupulously, if possible, than he does the bond a breach of which subjects him to legal liabilities; and the United States, in aiming to maintain itself as one of the most enlightened nations, would do its citizens gross injustice if it applied to its international relations any other than a high standard of honor and morality. On that ground the United States cannot properly be put in the position of countenancing a wrong after its commission any more than in that of consenting to it in advance.

It is needless to discuss here the circumstances and conditions that brought about later the annexation of these Islands to the United States, or to explain that if any wrong was done to the dethroned queen by such annexation, it seems to have been providentially overruled for the greater good of the Hawaiian people. These facts, however, cannot detract from our recognition and appreciation of the clear and discriminating statement of our ethical ideals as a nation that is contained in this message of Mr. Cleveland.

Theodore Roosevelt found many occasions in his public career to refer to the Christian religion as the inspiration and foundation of the highest civic and national morality. Many of his public utterances could be delivered with the utmost propriety from any Christian pulpit. Take as a specimen the following, which is but one among many similar utterances which came from him, to show the high estimate which he placed upon religion in the life of a nation:

> I cannot understand any American citizen who has the faintest feeling of patriotism and devotion to his country failing to appreciate the absolutely essential need of religion (using it in its broadest and deepest sense) to the welfare of this country. If it were not that in our villages and towns as they have grown up the Churches have grown in them, symbolizing the fact that there were among the foremost workers men whose work was not for the things of the body but for the things of the soul, this would not be a nation today; because this country would not be an abode fit for civilized men if it were not true that we put our material civilization, our material prosperity, as the base only upon which to build the superstructure of the higher spiritual life.

A man of clean, pure life and unblemished record, of unusually sturdy, robust, and manly Christian character, of lofty Christian ideals for himself as a ruler and for the people over whom he ruled, he was indeed an honor to the nation.

One other honored name will be mentioned later among the presidents who have helped to make a later epoch in history providential.

Chapter 5
Our Ethical Idealism And Altruism

Only that nation can consistently claim that an overruling Providence directed its origin, and that the Hand of God has been constantly manifest in its history, which continually brings forth deeds worthy of such a high claim. What deeds, now, can America appeal to in proof of the truth of her claim that she had a providential origin, and has had a providential history, and has a truly providential mission in the world? Surely such deeds only as bear the marks of a high standard of Christian ethics, and will bear the further and harder test of sincere and unquestioned altruism, can be named as worthy fruits of a tree that claims, like the vine from Egypt transplanted in Canaan, to have been planted by a Hand Divine. The noblest deeds both of men and of nations are often done in quietness and obscurity, un noticed in the ordinary round of life's incessant duties, the actors themselves being unconscious of anything save the conscientious discharge of duty. And this is none the less true because it is customary to cite (as we shall do) only such deeds as are conspicuous and well-known in stances and examples of high ethics and genuine altruism.

The spirit of America, of the real and true and ideal America, is best described by four words: faith, freedom, ethics, altruism—(1) faith that shows itself in recognizing and reverencing God's Providence; (2) freedom, both civil and religious, that never turns liberty to do good into license to do evil; (3) the ethical ideals of Christ the standard of conduct and character, not only for individuals, but for the nation as well, and (4) altruism that is made manifest in disinterested service for others. Altruism—using knowledge to help the ignorant, power to help the weak, wealth to help the poor, health to help the sick, and virtue to help the sinful—is a law of life, obligatory not more upon the individual than it is upon the nation; and in these righteous scales Jehovah weighs nations as well as individuals.

By these ethical standards let us judge our nation in the past, and determine our duty for the future. That much in our past history falls far short of this ethical ideal must be confessed. And yet this has been, and is, and must in the future be, our ideal—even though it be, as ideals always are, something that moves above and ahead, up to which the nation looks and toward which it ever moves as its goal.

Three notable episodes in our history may be referred to as peculiarly expressive of the real and true spirit of America, and as instances of our fully measuring up to the high ethical and altruistic ideal of the nation.

The motives that led the American people into the Spanish-American War were in the highest degree ethical and altruistic. Judged by the incidents and events of that war—the un broken series of victories on one side, and of defeats on the other—no war in biblical history, no war in all history, ever furnished more conspicuous evidence that Providence wrought for one nation and against the other, than was everywhere and all the time evident in this war. Evidence was never wanting that the Lord who loveth truth and righteousness, and the freedom which they alone can give, made his Providence to favor the nation that fought unselfishly for the rights of a downtrodden and unjustly oppressed people, But perhaps the finest exhibition of ethics and altruism that was furnished by that war, came when it was over, and the victorious nation had the conquered nation at its mercy. Did any nation ever do a finer, a more generous and magnanimous thing than to treat a conquered and prostrate nation as the United States treated Spain and her captive soldiers at the end of that war? It was then that America gave Spain and the world such an exhibition of genuine and generous altruism as no nation had ever furnished before, while, at the same time, it gave to Cuba her independence and the pledge of whatever financial and other help might be necessary for her national upbuilding. And this was done under conditions and circumstances that would have probably led any other conquering nation in the world to make this war the occasion for annexing Cuba to the United States, a thing which self-interest rendered most desirable but which the ethical and altruistic ideals of the American people pre vented us from doing.

Another deed worthy of a nation with a high moral ideal was furnished in the Chinese Boxer war, when the verdict of the foreign nations whose financial and other rights it was claimed had been invaded by the rebellious Boxers and not properly protected by the Chinese government, assessed enormous and, what many outsiders regarded as outrageously unjust, indemnities against China—and this was done in spite of America's insistent and unyielding protest. Then again came an opportunity, not indeed for magnanimity and generosity, but rather for simple ethics and justice on the part of America.

Out of the millions awarded our government by the foreign Powers that exercised jurisdiction in the case, our government paid reasonable compensation for damages done to Americans and their property, and then returned to China in a lump sum well-nigh all the millions that had been awarded to us—and in so acting America stood absolutely alone among the nations involved. Such unselfishness had its rich moral reward in the gratitude that was felt by the Chinese people for a deed so out of keeping with the prevailing diplomatic national custom and so in keeping with America's high standard of international ethics. It is not a matter for surprise that, following that memorable episode in our relations with the Chinese government, the hearts of the people of China should have become peculiarly open to Christian missionaries and teachers from America as well as to the representatives of our civil government. The money returned to them was used in a manner most agreeable both to China and to America, to educate a select number of Chinese young men and young women in American colleges and universities, all of whom in returning to their home land have borne back with them not only the good will of America, but the Christian ethical ideals of our people.

But during the century and a half that has elapsed since our nation began its career, there has been no epoch and no event in our history, and indeed in the history of the world, so momentous, and so demanding the exercise of high ethics and generous altruism on the part of men and nations, as the quadrennium[sic] embraced in the late world war (1914-1918) into which the voice of Divine Providence and a suffering world called our nation by many infallible signs and tokens, From the Declaration of Independence to the present time there has never been such an arousing of the moral consciousness of the American people, such a clear vision of simple, stern, inescapable duty, such singleness of aim and unity of action, such genuine altruism and self-forgetfulness, such a spirit of self-sacrifice, such enthusiasm for humanity, as characterized the people of the United States when in 1917, following what they believed to be the leadings of Divine Providence, they entered the world war and flung themselves with self-effacing abandon into the fight for human freedom—for the freedom of all nations and all men in all nations.

It may be that our nation should have heard and responded to the call of God and humanity sooner than it did. It may be that many of our people ignobly commercialized their patriotism and fought more to gain gold for themselves than to secure life and liberty for others. It may be that the demoralization and surging waves of selfishness and commercialism and lawlessness which have followed the war and engulfed our own and other nations, have made it hard to maintain that a really high and unselfish altruism ever did actuate us in entering the war. It may be that our people have had occasion to hang their heads in shame over what our nation has failed to do since the war ended. All this may be true. But no man can be true to the American people and to the facts of history, and say that our people were not as a whole actuated by the loftiest and most altruistic of motives when in 1917, with their hearts beating as the heart of one, they went into that awful struggle across the sea, believing that it was no less a part of their providential mission as a nation to make this fight for humanity their own than was the fight for their independence in 1776, or for the preservation of the Union and the abolition of slavery in 1862. Dr. Henry Churchill King has shown that not only all true Americans but many representatives of other nations also were quick to recognize and declare the truth and justice of these statements concerning America's altruism in this war:

> There is no mistaking the rare and lofty idealism with which America entered this war. America made her decision to enter the war on high ethical and essentially Christian grounds. Not for territorial or commercial gains; abjuring all idea of later indemnities; practically unmoved, it must be stated, by thoughts even of self-defense; after every righteous effort to preserve peaceful relations with Germany had been exhausted; when the greatness of the issues had become plain; in the face of fixed American traditions; in marvelously unified fashion; and across three thousand miles of sea—America threw her whole self,

with every resource, into this struggle, for the sake of righteousness, of humanity, of civilization. It was a singularly impressive moral movement. No wonder that the distinguished litterateur, Hughes de Roux, voiced his conviction by declaring that *"history had never before seen a great nation moved to war by so completely unselfish and idealistic motives"*; nor that Mr. Balfour should describe the entry of the United States into the war as *"the most magnificent and generous act in all history."* *"And they came,"* said Henry Bergson, the noted French philosopher, *"with no designing aim, stirred neither by selfish interest nor by fear, but by a principle, by an ideal, by the thought of the mission they were called upon to fulfill in the world."*

But, lest America should be exalted above measure and be filled with pride and self-esteem because of her own altruism, Providence, quickly after the war, suffered days of disillusionment and retrogression to come to the nation—days which, whether it should be so or not, have sadly discounted and discredited, in the eyes of all nations, the high claims made for ethical ideal ism and altruism on the part alike of our soldiers abroad and our people at home preceding and accompanying our participation in the war. But even days of disillusionment have a providential mission and teach a needed lesson that will not be learned in any other way, and that is, that lofty ethical idealism will not remain in the high air of itself, and that altruism will not remain disinterested and unselfish of itself. The same moral free will and personal power that called them into existence are necessary to keep them in existence. When the engine that took the aeroplane on high ceases to furnish power, engine and airplane fall to earth, When the heart ceases to send forth its currents of blood throughout the body, the heart and body die, Eternal vigilance is the price not only of liberty but of all progress; and moral progress is something which, however providential it be, is yet conditioned on human cooperation: it will not take care of itself. The keeping up of the never-ending fight necessary to hold what has been gained in moral progress, and to keep the progress perpetually progressing, is the great problem of Christian civilization in periods of peace. To win this ceaseless fight for moral progress, and keep it won, demands nothing less than a full moral equivalent of war. However justifiable a nation's entrance into a given war may be, and no matter how ethical and altruistic its motives, it must not be forgotten that moral progress is the achievement of peace and not of war.

Peace, then, and not war is the best testing period of ethics and altruism in a nation, and furnishes the best opportunity for their cultivation and exercise. The nation has been great in ethics and altruism in time of war; it should be greater still in times of peace.

It is not wise, as a rule, to attempt to interpret any man's life and work as they are related to providential history until he is dead and his work is done. But we cannot close this study of the Hand of God in our history without referring to one President who is yet living. The man who voiced the sentiments of the American people and led the nation in the late world-war crisis in our history, out of the shadows and perils of which we have not even yet passed, is destined, we believe, to take and to hold a permanent place in the front rank of those providential leaders that have made our nation morally great in the past and upon whose leader ship the nation must depend in no small degree for great moral achievements in the future.

Woodrow Wilson seemed, in the providence of God, to have *"come to the kingdom for a time like this,"* and coming years will not diminish but deepen the world's appreciation of the great service he rendered our own and other nations at this moral crisis in the history of nations. Many of his public utterances during the eventful years of 1914-1919, when he was the moral leader and spokesman not only of the American people, but of multiplied millions in other lands, are worthy to be placed, along with those of Washington, Jefferson, Lincoln, and Cleveland, among the official documents and state papers which we must rely upon to prove the truth of the claim that we are here making that God has blessed us above all other nations in giving us God-fearing and divinely guided men as leaders and rulers, and that, under the leadership vouchsafed to us by Providence, our nation has been called to fill in the past, and is called yet more fully to fill in the future, an altogether unique, important, and responsible mission among the nations of the earth.

Among the many utterances of President Wilson expressing our ethical idealism as a nation we quote the following, each paragraph being taken from a different address, but all of them characterized by a common idea that brings them into unity in setting forth the ethical ideal of the American nation:

If America stands for one thing more than for another, it is for the sovereignty of self-governing people, and her example, her assistance, and her encouragement have thrilled two continents in this Western world with all those fine impulses which have built up human liberty on both sides of the water. She stands, therefore, as an example of independence, as an example of free institutions, and as an example of disinterested inter national action in the maintenance of justice.

Why is it that every nation turns to us with the instinctive feeling that if anything touches humanity it touches us? Because it knows that ever since we were born as a nation, we have undertaken to be the champions of humanity and the rights of men. Without that ideal there would be nothing that would distinguish America from her predecessors in the history of nations.

But the final test of the validity, the strength, the irresistible force of the American ideal has now come. The rest of the world must be made to realize from this time on just what America stands for; and, when that happy time comes when peace shall reign again, and America shall take part in the undisturbed and unclouded counsels of the world, it will be realized that the promises of the fathers, and the ideals of the men who thought nothing of their lives in comparison with their ideals, will have been vindicated, and the world will say: *"America promised to hold this light of liberty and right up for the guidance of our feet, and behold she has redeemed her promise. Her men, her leaders, her rank and file, are pure of heart; they have purged their hearts of selfish ambition, and they have said to all mankind: Men and brethren, let us live together in righteousness and in the peace which springeth only from the soil of righteousness itself."*

And my dream is this: that as the years go on and the world knows more and more of America, it will also drink at these fountains of youth and renewal, that it will also turn to America for those moral inspirations that lie at the base of human freedom, that no nation will ever fear America unless it finds itself engaged in some enterprise inconsistent with the rights of humanity, and that America will come into the full light of that day when all shall know that she puts human rights above all other rights, and that her flag Is the flag not only of America but the flag of humanity Ex-President Wilson's latest published utterance closes with these significant words: *"The sum of the whole matter is this—that our civilization cannot survive materially unless it is re deemed spiritually. It can be saved only by becoming permeated with the spirit of Christ and being made free and happy by the practices which spring out of that spirit. Only thus can discontent be driven out, and all the shadows lifted from the road ahead. Here is the final challenge to our Churches, to our political organizations and to our capitalists—to everyone who fears God or loves his country."* (Atlantic Monthly, August, 1923.)

The final results accomplished by the recent *"Disarmament Conference"* held at the invitation of our Government in the city of Washing ton are not yet ready for appraisement, but are even now sufficiently apparent to justify us in feeling that the leadership of our nation in bringing about and promoting the work of this conference are in keeping with our traditional record, ethical and altruistic, which commits us to using our influence and best offices for promoting peace among all nations. But America, if she be true to the ethical ideals of the past, will not be content to stop with this effort for world peace.

The late President Warren G. Harding, though speaking as a political leader and statesman, uttered truths worthy of a prophet of righteousness, when he said shortly before he died, that *"the only sure cure for many of the ills of the modern world which men are vainly trying to remove by means of social and economic anti dotes is to be found in faith in God and loyalty to the eternal verities of religion. The recognition of a personal God and of the individual accountability of men and women to him, for their conduct are the foundations of the highest patriotism and of those civic virtues which alone can make men and nations morally great. The human race has been getting away from its religious moorings. It needs a revival of the sincere conception of the personal relationship of God to man and man to God; a restoration of faith in the fundamentals of religion that are eternal. The world needs the assurance of faith in the Almighty, and the tranquility which comes alone of that faith. That faith in God which made the ancient Hebrew nation great, is still needed to make nations great today."*

"The Master is come, and calleth for thee," are words that may be as fittingly addressed to a nation today as they were to the young woman of Bethany in the lifetime of our Lord; and the things to which He calls cannot be misunderstood by any one that hears his voice. It is to altruistic service, not to isolation and self-centeredness, that God calls the America of his Providence. This great nation, the helm of whose history his Hand has guided in the past, cannot be true to its divine call in this new day of world needs and world opportunities, if it closes its ears to the cry of the nations and its eyes to the vision of their needs. If famine, or pestilence, or flood, or earthquake, or any other disaster has befallen the people of any land at

any time, the American government and people have never failed to do the ethical, altruistic, and generous thing as needed. The gift of money and of men and women for helpful and sacrificial service, whenever and wherever needed, has always answered without delay the call of humanity—and this to such an extent that America has become the synonym among all nations for generosity and helpfulness. This is as it should be; and this is the best proof of the presence of God's Hand in our history. Nor should the commercialism and profiteering of money-loving and money-making men in our country be allowed to blind any man's eyes to the recognition of the splendid altruism that belongs, and has always belonged, to our people.

Nowhere else in all the world have so many men and women of great wealth turned their accumulated millions into the service of humanity at home and abroad, as here in America. Whenever anything is to be done in the world, two things are necessary, money and men. Money is needed and much of it, and needed for everything; and this means that it is the duty and providential mission of some men and some nations to make it, to make it that it may be used for the service of humanity. The commercialism whose accumulated coin is turned into currency for the service of mankind is in its ultimate aim ethical and altruistic. If America controls the wealth of the world, and is herself ruled by gold, it is the providential mission of her ethical idealism and altruism to turn this rule of gold into the golden rule.

A great nation has never perhaps in the history of the world had so great an opportunity, by virtue of its unprecedented possession both of wealth and of moral influence, to practice with generous altruism the golden rule and the law of love toward unfortunate and suffering sister nations as has the American nation today. Not only is it true that *"man's extremity is God's opportunity,"* but it is also true that the world's extremity is a Christian nation's great opportunity to serve mankind and bless the world by giving practical proof that the golden rule and the law of love can be practiced by nations as truly as by individuals. It was in the darkest days of Hebrew history that prophetic optimism and universalism burst into glorious song, inspired by the vision of the coming Messiah; and in and through the Hebrew nation the Messiah came in spite of the wreck and ruin of empires that seemed for the time to make vain all hope and promise of his coming. Happy would we be if America might become the servant of Jehovah in this our day through whom the Messiah's golden rule and law of love should be made real in the world. It was with America's opportunity for this Messianic service in mind that the following lines were written:

> Whene'er with faith we dare to hold
> That golden rule, not rule of gold,
> Shall be for men and nations, too,
> The rule of life the whole world through;
>
> When rich and poor alike shall see
> From golden rule no man is free;
> When greed of gold and jealous hate,
> Overcome by love, and shame, abate;
>
> When we dare seek with all our heart
> To serve all men, and do our part
> Through love that shares in generous deed,
> And joys to meet another's need;
>
> Then earth will see the day at hand
> When all true souls in every land
> In league of love for right shall stand;
>
> When all one golden rule shall own,
> And love on earth shall claim the throne,
> And Love in heaven as God be known.
>
> For faith can never know defeat
> That has In power of love its seat.

(Nashville Christian Advocate, November 28, 1919.)

Chapter 6
What Makes A Nation Great?

What, then, shall we say, in view of these facts, is the vocation of the American nation? What is the task which Providence has assigned to us as a people, discharging which we will fill our place among those favored nations who are *"the called according to God's purpose"* — called to serve, not themselves only, but others also, and perchance all mankind? We answer our own question in language partly furnished by one of our own great Presidents: It is our mission to maintain in the world that form of government which is best adapted to promoting the highest good of all its citizens, intellectually, morally, and socially; to lift needless and unnatural burdens from all shoulders; to clear the paths of all worthy and laudable pursuits and throw them open to all who are prepared to enter them, and to afford all an unfettered start, and as far as government can make it so, a fair and equal chance to achieve success in the race of life. And then, having done this for its own people—indeed, while doing this for its own people—to use its moral influence and material power to secure similar conditions and advantages for all other peoples without regard to race or residence.

The final proof of the Hand of God in a nation's history then is not found, if this answer be true, in its unequaled wealth, or its commercial supremacy, or political prestige or military power, but in the moral metal of its manhood and the moral worth of its womanhood—in the goodness and greatness of its people. *"Ye shall know the truth, and the truth shall make you free"*—knowledge, truth, freedom, personality— these are the things provided by Providence to make individuals and nations great. And when this greatness has been attained, *"he that is greatest among you shall be the servant of all"* — this is the test and proof of greatness in the eyes of God for nations as well as for individuals. Knowledge and culture, ethics and character, service and altruism, personality and power— these are the credentials furnished by God to men and nations who, submitting to his providential guidance, seek for honor and glory and immortality.

The American sage and philosopher who furnished the words with which we began our study of God's Hand in our history at its beginning, has no less happily described for us the providential aim and end of that history in a little poem titled "*The Nation's Strength,*" which needs often to be quoted that it may alike warn us of our danger and inspire us to seek for national greatness and glory where alone it is to be found:

> What builds a nation's pillars high
> And its foundations strong?
> What makes it mighty to defy
> The foes that round it throng?
>
> It is not gold. Its kingdoms grand
> Go down in battle's shock; Its shafts are laid on sinking sand,
> Not on abiding rock.
>
> Is it the sword? Ask the red dust
> Of empires passed away;
> The blood has turned their stones to rust,
> Their glory to decay.
>
> And is it pride? Ah, that bright crown
> Has aeemed to nations sweet;
> But God has struck its luster down
> In ashes at his feet.
> Not gold, but only men can make
> A people great and strong,
> Men who for truth and honor's sake
> Stand fast and suffer long.
>
> Brave men who work while others sleep,
> Who dare while others fly—
> They build a nation's pillars deep
> And lift them to the sky.

(Copyrighted by Houghton, Mifflin & Company. Printed by permission.)

There can be no more fitting time than now to quote the following remarkable words from Alexis de Tocqueville, famous statesman and historian of France and author of *"Democracy in America,"* in four volumes, of which work the Edinburgh Review, many years after its first appearance, said: *"Far from having suffered from the lapse of time, it has gained in authority and interest, and this because of the inexhaustible depth, the unflinching truth, and the extraordinary foresight which are its characteristics"*:

> I sought for the greatness and genius of America in her commodious harbors and her ample rivers and it was not there. I sought for the greatness and genius of America in her fertile fields and boundless forests and it was not there. I sought for the greatness and genius of America in her rich mines and her vast world commerce and it was not there. I sought for the greatness and genius of America in her public school system and her institutions of learning and it was not there. I sought for the greatness and genius of America in her democratic congress and her matchless Constitution and it was not there. Not until I went into the churches of America and heard her pulpits flame with righteousness did I understand the secret of her genius and power, America is great because America is good, and if America ever ceases to be good, America will cease to be great.

Only in case we seek and find the strength and greatness of our nation in the things of which Ralph Waldo Emerson sings and the great French author writes will the *"Ship of State,"* of which Longfellow wrote, bear a cargo of men and women worthy of the *"Master who laid the keel"* and of the Pilot who has never left the helm:

> Sail on, sail on, O Ship of State!
> Sail on, O Union, strong and great!
> Humanity, with all its fears,
> With all the hopes of future years,
> Is hanging breathless on thy fate!
>
> We know what Master laid thy keel,
> What Workman wrought thy ribs of steel,
> Who made each mast and sail and rope,
> What anvils rang, what hammers beat,
> In what a forge and what a heat
> Were shaped the anchors of thy hope!
>
> Sail on, nor fear to breast the sea!

Our hearts, our hopes are all with thee,
Our hearts, our hopes, our prayers, our tears,
Our faith triumphant o'er our fears,
Are all with thee—are all with thee!

Book Two
The Hand of God in American History

By
John F. Bigelow
Pastor of Keeseville Baptist Church

A Discourse Delivered in the Baptist Church, Keeseville, NY
July 7, 1861

Also Before The United Literary Societies of New Hampton Institution,
Fairfax, VT, July 15, 1861

Chapter One
Chapter Two 44
Chapter Three 52
Chapter Four 58
Chapter Five 63
Chapter Six 68

DISCOURSE

Chapter One

If we look into the History of Nations, we shall find that not a few of them supposed themselves to be the special favorites of Divine Providence. If we inquire also into the state of national feeling, as it now exists in different countries, we shall find, in numbers of them, no lack of present evidences of the same assumption.

I hardly need to say, so obvious is the truth, that in general the source of such an impression has been and is, an overweening national vanity. Were it necessary to furnish illustrations of this feeling, we could point not only to Ancient Greece and Rome, whose real superiority might be some justification of their exalted self-estimate; but we could point to the line of the proud Pharaohs, and to almost every Asiatic nation, whether of the past or of the present, particularly to China and Japan, whose matchless conceit utters itself in grandiloquence most pompously and ineffably absurd; we could point to the subjects of the Russian Autocrat, to the valorous but boastful sons of Gaul and Britain, and find in each of these examples of national arrogance. Nor are these all; if the statements of Historians and Travelers are to be credited, we could refer to some of even the most inconsiderable and abject tribes, and find among them specimens of vain-glory as inordinate, and of self-conceit as supercilious as are anywhere to be found. Entertaining such exaggerated views of its own importance, it is but natural that each of these nations should regard itself as a special object of Providential interest, and therefore as possessing a special History.

That the Jews regarded their history as peculiar and even unparalleled, is evident because they said so: "*He hath not so dealt with any nation.*" Nor will anyone, who is acquainted with the facts of their history, regard such a view, on their part, as an assumption. Does the story of other nations tell of remarkable events, of hairbreadth escapes, of wonderful deliverances, of daring exploits and grand achievements? The annals of the Israelites relate those, the equal of which veritable history nowhere else records, and which the most romantic legend has hardly surpassed.

In the case of the American people, as in that of the Jews, we believe that it is no dictate of national vanity, when we claim that God has given us a history unique and peculiar: when we claim that "*He hath not so dealt with any nation.*"

Accordingly the subject, on which I propose to address you at this time is, the Hand of God in American History.

I. In the first place, let me point you to some of the manifestations and developments of peculiar Providential agency in our historical career.

1. At the outset, one illustration of God's Providence working in our history, and one which should not be overlooked, I find in the character and peculiarities of the country to which our ancestors were conducted, and which, as a nation, we occupy.

No one, who is at all acquainted with the labors of Ritter, Humboldt, Gnyot and others in the department of physical study, will fail to recognize the relations of Geography to History; no such one, we think, will doubt, that the structure of Continents has an important part to perform in the education and development of nations. Divine Providence has assigned to every historical people a special geographical locality, thus determining *"the bounds of their habitation."* As it was therefore with t he great Empires of the East, as it was in later days with Greece and Rome, as it is now with the nations of modern Europe, so have we received a geographical position appropriate to our character and historical functions as a People. Accordingly it was not an inconsiderable island like England or Ireland, which God had prepared as the refuge and home of the exiled Puritans.

It was not some pent-up nook of Europe already occupied, and even swarming with nations, where they would be hemmed in by jealous and encroaching neighbors. It was not a country like Switzerland, to which God sent our ancestors; a country which, though beautiful by its sweet valleys, and sublime by its Alps and Glaciers, is nevertheless limited in extent, surrounded on all sides by dominant nations, and without outlet to the sea, by which, through commerce and navigation, it could go forth to influence the world. It was not to such as these, but to a widely extended continent, which, however it may have been visited by Scandinavian navigators in distant centuries, was kept hidden from the civilized world until the close of the fifteenth century; God thus preserving it from the occupancy of rapacious gold-seekers, adventurous Colonists and ambitious Kings; it was, to a continent possessing an adapted soil and climate, a land rich in vegetable productions and mineral resources; it was to a land whose coast is indented with numerous bays and harbors, thus fitting it for foreign commerce, and whose broad lakes and long rivers afford the most extensive facilities for inland navigation; it was to a country exhibiting every variety of natural aspect, from the wildest mountain scenery to the most pleasing rural landscape; to a country stretching from the Atlantic to the Pacific, from the frigid regions of the British Provinces in the north, to the sunny plains of Mexico in the south; to a country of which large portions are so fertile, that it may be called the garden of the world; while the principal part of the remainder yields to labor, bringing forth, by skillful cultivation, abundantly, or at least sufficiently, for all the exigencies [problems requiring immediate action] of a vigorous, working population; it was to a country furnishing facilities to the frugal, industrious and energetic, and it ought to furnish them to no others, for almost every kind of business and pursuit, agricultural, manufacturing and commercial; it was to one whose *"characteristic is simplicity, unity,"** the last of the *"three historical continents;"* it was to a land forming an indivisible domain, *"where all the peoples of Europe may meet together with room enough to move in, may commingle their efforts and their gifts, and carry out upon a scale of grandeur hitherto unknown, the life-giving principle of modern times, the principle of free association."* (* Guyot's *Earth and Man*, Page 297.)

Such is the country to which Divine Providence led our forefathers in order to plant this great nation.

Nor was it unwittingly and blindly that he conveyed them here. It was to such a country that he led them, a land so ample, so distinguished by natural advantages that our people might be, to a great degree, independent or self-dependent; that our population might be numerous; that it might be in the main homogeneous; that our nationality might be bold, strong and influential; that our numerous citizens, occupying one compact and connected territory, might be formed under the same influences ; that they might live under the same government and institutions, both civil and religious; and that thus living on one connected soil, and thus subjected to one class of influences, instead of being dispersed as distant and dissimilar provincials, they might become essentially component parts of one great social and political unity. Had our population been scattered in remote dependences, or had that population been numerically small, we should have had neither the assimilated character nor the aggregate substance for strong national influence. God then has given us an ample and consolidated country, for in numbers and identity of character, are to be found the materials and forces of our national power, political and moral.

Chapter Two

2. Another development of God's Providence, as dealing peculiarly with our nation, is to be found in the Colonial period of its history.

God is in history, and he who fails to discover Him in it, does not read it rightly: does not seize and appreciate its true spirit. To prove these statements is no part of my work at this time, for I regard myself as speaking not to skeptics, but to believers in the doctrine of Divine Providence. I repeat then, God through Christ is in all history ; and Pie is in it working out great principles. At every evolution He exhibits some important truth; ne is in it all, advancing the great objects of human good and His own glory.

I do not mean to say, however, that the process of historical development proceeds directly forward without interruption. I do not mean to say that the stream of history flows ever onward, encountering no obstacles, describing no meandering movements. Temporary suspensions there may be, or at least they appear to be. Such an apparent suspension there was of the great development of history in the mediaeval Ages. During this long period there was little apparent advancement. God's purposes, however, even then, were doubtless advancing towards their maturity, though by a hidden process; and that period, as well as previous and succeeding ones, subserved [useful], without doubt, some end in the far-reaching economy of His designs; just as winter with all its snow, ice and cold is conducive to vegetation. Though there is the outward semblance of death, Nature is not then dead nor inactive; she is elaborating those juices, and going forward with those processes that are essential to the beauty and verdure of the following spring. Accordingly there is reason to believe that the winter of the dark Ages was not totally lost time as regards the prosecution of God's great purposes in human history.

The argument, moreover, is not one from analogy merely. That this period had its uses, however dreary and barren it may seem to us, is probable also because the human mind was not then torpid. Though seemingly fruitless in important results, yet its action was oftentimes intense. Do you inquire for the proof of this? You have only to study the history of scholasticism; you have only to feel the mental pulse of such men as Peter Lombard, Albert the Great, Thomas Aquinas, Duns Scotus and William Occam; you have only to witness that sturdy, intellectual gladiatorship, which appears in the contests of the Nominalists and Realists. Though their philosophy may be characterized and perhaps justly as *"scholastic subtilty"* and *"scholastic trifling,"* yet there was in it intense thinking. Nor was that thinking merely abstract and metaphysical, it was practical and religious. Tendencies had long been astir, looking to a new order of things. As the dawn comes before the day, announcing and ushering it in; as some mild days precede the spring softening the rigors of winter and preparing for the vernal change, so the Reformation had its precursors and preparatives. Ullmann, indeed, has given the Christian world a history of the *"Reformers before the Reformation."*

By and by, however, the *"fulness of time"* had come, and the scene changes. Borrowing the idea of Schwegler, when Nominalism had separated thought from being, and divorced the theological from the practical, then the religious consciousness of the age broke with the traditional dogma, which rupture constituted the Reformation. The long winter of Mediaeval Scholasticism and Catholicism broke up when the spring of the Reformation, previously heralded, actually came. Then the ice and snow melted away, or rather much of it melted, for it is sad to see, that, on the soil of the Reformation, one encounters still not infrequent masses of traditional ice, which the sun of Protestantism has not yet dissolved. At the Reformation, however, the human mind, so long comparatively stationary, started forward by a surprising progress. Yet that progress, great as it was, was far in the rear of the point which has been reached by the Christian civilization of to- day.

The Reformation dates back almost to the period when Columbus discovered the new world. Luther had discovered, too, a new world in Theology; and these two events, the most important in modern times, are intimately connected in their bearings upon American history. The God of Providence had thus connected them, in order to bring out, according to His own plan, the development of His purposes.

Yet, though the Reformation was thus early in its occurrence, and thus important in its character, it did not, as already intimated, reach its present stage of advancement until after the tardy lapse of years. The steps of constitutional liberty have always been slow, because its course has always been an up-hill one. Long was it before the idea of complete religions freedom was attained. Hence, even down to the latter half of the seventeenth century, we find the Church of England publishing the acts of uniformity, thus driving from her bosom hundreds and thousands of the best of her sons, both Ministers and Laymen. It is only to indicate the spirit of the age, and not for purposes of sectarian depreciation, that we allude to this fact.

The Reformation, however, was destined to advance a second step, appearing under & purer form, and on a different soil. To escape from religious intolerance, a body of English Dissenters, reproachfully termed Puritans, were seen flying first to Holland, and then to these American shores, which Providence, by means of the Genoese navigator, had opened just before the dawn of the Reformation, as a theatre on which to make a new development of the Christian and social economy. God had prepared this western wilderness as an asylum for liberty and religion, escaping from the persecution and oppression of the Old World. Thus exiled and escaping, Divine Providence watched and guided their flight. He preserved the Mayflower in her perilous passage. At length He gave to that intrepid company upon her deck, to land upon the rock of Plymouth. By means of a pestilence, which had cut off large numbers of the aboriginal inhabitants, He had already prepared a place for them, to which the friendly Samoset bade them welcome. Winter reigned with its stern rigors. Sickness and death were abroad in their ranks. Carver, chosen before they landed, to be their Governor, was, together with his sons and wife, already in his grave. A Historian of the Colony tells us that, *"at one time, every person in the settlement except seven, was on a sick bed."* Withal, the hostility of the savages hourly threatened their destruction; for, although the Wampanoags entered into a friendly treaty with them, the Narragansetts looked upon them as intruders. In token of the doom which they might expect, Canonicus sends to Badford, the successor of Carver, a bundle of arrows wrapped in a rattle-snake's skin.

Under circumstances such as these, what could there be before them, but speedy destruction? To the human eye, what prospect could be gloomier? What other dark prognostic is needed to foreshadow their fate? Yet strange to say all auguries fail here; all principles of human calculation, for once, prove false. And why? because God's Providence comes in among them disturbing and arranging to suit its own ends. That little band of Pilgrims are preserved because God has great uses to make of them in future history. Hence neither cold nor sickness nor starvation were permitted utterly to waste them, nor the savages to cut them off. Though by these destroying agents their numbers were greatly thinned, yet God did not suffer them to become extinct. Through these Puritans He intended to realize, in the form of permanent institutions, ideas of religion and government which the majority of mankind but imperfectly understood, which they were poorly prepared to appreciate, and which they were but little disposed to promote, but which, being essential to the true development of humanity, were wrapped up in the Divine purposes. A decade of years passed on; Salem, Charlestown, Dorchester, Roxbury, Watertown, Cambridge and Boston, are settled; trade is opening with the mother country; the foundations of a permanent Colony are laid.

Such is the beginning of our national history. It was the Puritanic element, which supplied the characteristic spirit in our civilization. True it is that as early as 1607, a settlement was formed in Virginia; but it was not of a material fit for use in God's plan of American History. Says Bancroft, "it was not the will of God that the new State should be formed of such material; that such men should be the fathers of a progeny born on the American soil, who were one day to assert American liberty by their eloquence and defend it by their valor." About the time, however, of the landing of the Pilgrims, the Virginia Colony had so changed in substance, that it was adapted to become an organic part of our historical development. The population of New Netherlands, New Sweden and Pennsylvania either was already sufficiently assimilated, or soon became enough so to enter, as constituent elements, into our American Nationality.

Looking back now over the century that had elapsed since 1517, and calling to mind the state of things then existing in Europe, we see that encouraging progress had indeed been made. Still some of those principles, which began to be evolved at the time of Luther, had as yet been but very imperfectly wrought out. Among these was that of religious Liberty. Should any of my observations at this point seem to detract a little from the full meed [reward] of praise sometimes given to the Puritans, I need only to reply, that they were men of a style of character so rich in noble qualities and manly virtues, that they can afford the statement of whatever deficiencies appeared in them, better perhaps than any class of men, of which history informs us. Some panegyrists of theirs have seemed to think it necessary to defend them from every possible charge of defect, fearing that otherwise their reputation will suffer; but they need not such defenders. The Puritans were men, if there are any such, whose reputation will take care of itself.

Much was gained for religious Liberty, when Luther first "broke" with the traditional dogmatism of the Papal Church: much was gained again when the Puritans "broke" with the Churchly authority, which they had left in England. A third "break" was now needed; and it was one with themselves. The principle of religious Liberty remaining still in a backward state, required a clear elimination and a decisive statement. To effect this there must be another exodus from religious intolerance, not indeed across an ocean: not to a foreign shore; but from one portion of our American soil to another.

The man to meet this emergency was Roger Williams: a man of noble type, of singular magnanimity, of conscientious firmness, of intrepid spirit, and though not without his defects, yet of remarkable breadth and vigor of moral and intellectual character, and in some respects entitled to stand as the foremost man of his time. For the sake of freedom to follow the course of his earnest and independent convictions of religious duty, he must fly from Massachusetts into the depths of the wilderness. After many perils escaped, after many privations and sufferings endured, after fourteen weeks of forest wanderings through the snows of a hard winter, *"not knowing what bread or bed did men,"* yet watched by the eye, and guided and girded by the hand of that Providence, which was fitting him for his work, he became, in 1636, the Founder of the State of Rhode Island.

Thus this Pioneer of religious Liberty established that Commonwealth, which, first of all the Governments on the face of the globe, furnished an example of unconditional toleration in matters of Religion. Thus he realized, for the first time, that grand idea—the freedom of religious opinion,—the carrying out of- which has not been the sole distinction of the State where it originated, but in respect to the rest of the world, has become the peculiar glory of the country of which that little State forms territorially so inconsiderable a part. The eye that sees no indications of a Divine Providence working in these historical developments is one which, though it can *"discern the face of the sky,"* cannot *"discern the signs of the times."* So deeply was Roger Williams impressed with such an Agency in his affairs, that, in recognition of it, the settlement which he had just founded he called Providence.

The germs of the National life already begin to appear; the tree of Liberty is taking root. Harvard College was soon instituted, *"which exerted a powerful influence in forming the early character of the country"*; and in respect to which, since it was the first educational expression of the Nation's intellectual spirit, of which our many other honored Colleges and Literary Institutions are also a product, they might say, without any self-detraction, she is *"the Mother of us all."* The foundation of our Common School system was soon laid *"to the end,"* in the language of the Puritans, *"that learning might not be buried in the graves of their forefathers."* It was ordered in all the Colonies *"that every township, after the Lord hath increased them to the number of fifty householders, shall appoint one to teach all children to write and read."* (Bancroft, Vol. 1, page 458.)

An American Literature, today, by no means limited in amount, nor contemptible in quality, had its origin among those earliest sources of our History. Says Bancroft: "The Press began its work in 1639." Then arose that system of Legislation, which, though not always broad in its principles, nor wise in its policy, did much in molding the national character, and which subsequently developed itself into the form of our free Government and free Institutions.

Thus do we see Divine Providence planting the seeds of this great Nation in the establishment of the Colonies; and evidences equally clear of its working, do we find in their subsequent growth and preservation. I may not dwell upon the hostility of the savages, surrounding them, and the frequent attacks from that source, which they were enabled to resist and suppress; for the lack of time forbids the delay; but I cannot forbear an allusion to a still more imminent peril from which they were preserved, I mean that of the threatened domination of the French and subjection to the power of the Pope. Had our forefathers failed here, how different would have been the whole course of American History. Who can estimate what, in that event, would have been the political, the intellectual and the moral differences? Especially, may we ask, who can conceive what would have been the religious difference.

Instead of a free Protestant religion and a free Church, we should have had a Roman hierarchy, with all its direful concomitants and consequents,—a State Church, a corrupt priesthood and an ignorant people. French Jesuits were ever busy, seeking to stir up the Indians to whet the knife and the tomahawk for the destruction of the Colonists. The French had a strong cordon of forts and defenses, extending from Nova Scotia and the banks of the St. Lawrence by Champlain and the Western Lakes, down the Ohio and the Mississippi, to Texas; and more than once, to the human eye, seemed likely to overrun the whole country. What murders they ruthlessly committed, what desolations they wrought on our unprotected frontiers, what wars they waged to obtain the object of their rapacious desires, our bloody Colonial History, in sad detail, full well informs us. It tells us of King William's war, of Queen Anne's war, of King George's war, of the French and Indian war.

Our narrow limits will allow no reference to the particular events of these dark struggles beyond the mention of a case noticed by Dr. Dwight, and cited by the writer of an admirable article in the Bibliotheca Sacra, as illustrating the "*Relation of Divine Providence to Physical Laws.*"[1] Dr. Dwight adduced it as an exemplification of Providential interference in answer to prayer. The case is that of the destruction of the French Armament under the Duke D'Anville in the year 1746, and which, he adds, "*ought to be remembered with gratitude and admiration by every inhabitant of this country. This fleet consisted of forty ships of war: was destined for the destruction of New England: was of sufficient force to render that destruction in the ordinary progress of things certain; and sailed from Chebucto,* [sic] *in Nova Scotia, for that purpose.*"[2] The writer of the article above alluded to proceeds to quote as follows from the "*History of the Old South Church, Boston.*" "*In the mean time,*" adds Dr. Wiener, "*our pious fathers, apprized of their danger, and feeling that their only safety was in God, had appointed a season of fasting and prayer, to be observed in all their Churches. While Mr. Prince was officiating (in the Old South Church of Boston, says a writer in the Columbian Sentinel of 1821,) on this fast day, and praying most fervently to God, to avert the dreaded calamity, a sudden gust of wind arose (the day had, till now, been perfectly clear and calm) so violent as to cause a loud clattering of the windows. The reverend pastor paused in his prayer; and looking around upon the congregation with a countenance of hope, he again commenced, and with great devotional ardor supplicated the Almighty to cause that wind to frustrate the object of our enemies, and save the country from Conquest and Popery. A tempest ensued, in which the greater part of the French fleet was wrecked on the coast of Nova Scotia. The Duke D'Anville, the principal General, and the second in command both committed suicide. Many died with disease, and thousands were consigned to a watery grave. The small number who remained alive, returned to France without health, and without spirits. And the enterprise was abandoned, and never again resumed.*"[3] The author of our article says in relation to this, and we concur in his view, "that the destruction of property and life was an answer to prayer, that the rising of any particular wave of the sea, or particular "gust of wind" was the result of a particular supplication therefore, we need not be confident; but that the safety of the Lord's heritage in New England, which was the supplicated favor, was vouchsafed in compliance with the supplication, we may rationally believe. The analogies of Divine Providence warrant the belief.

[1] We presume that the author is Prof. Park.
[2] *Theology*, Vol. V, Page 40.
[3] *Bib. Sacra*, Jan. No. 1855, Page 187.

Chapter Three

3. Another field for the exemplification of God's Providence, as acting and guiding in our Nation's affairs, is to be found in the *Revolutionary Period* of our History.

I am not about to discuss the somewhat casuistic principle of political revolutions. "While, however, I accept firmly the scriptural doctrine that Government is an Institution of God, and therefore for no slight causes is to be overthrown, or even resisted; yet at the same time I believe just as firmly, that it is possible for a Government to reach a stage of abuses so aggravated, that when all legal methods for the redress of grievances have been tried in vain, then it is right for the oppressed to seek the redress of their wrongs by Revolution. Still, though this is a right of the down-trodden, yet it is always the ultimate right; and each case of attempted revolution is to be judged of by itself, receiving approval or condemnation, according to its character, from that principle of justice which is common to, at least, the better portion of mankind, and which is analagons [sic] to that other principle in Man, denominated, in both ordinary speech and philosophic terminology, *"common sense."* The Fathers of our Republic recognized - this principle.

When, therefore, they were about to dissolve the *"political bands,"* which connected them with the Mother Country, they said that *"a decent respect for the opinions of mankind required that they should declare the causes which impelled them to the separation."* Accordingly in the Declaration of Independence they set those causes forth. These, as they stand in that Instrument, mankind have had before them for nearly a century: men have formed their judgment upon them; and I have no hesitancy in asserting, that the better "opinions of mankind" have always approved, and will always approve them. The justifications of the American Revolution I shall leave, therefore, where the Framers of the Declaration of Independence left them, that is, with the judgment and conscience of universal humanity.

Nay, I go farther than this. I affirm that the American Revolution was a historical necessity, in virtue of its being an organic part of a plan which God had begun to develop on the shores of the New World; a plan having respect to the highest interests of the human race for the Ages, and the whole Kingdom of God on earth.

Do you ask me for the proof of such a plan? I judge it sufficient for a reply to appeal to the position which this Nation has held, and the function which it has fulfilled, in view of the nations and peoples of the earth, from the day of its acknowledged independence to the present hour. It has been, in all its history, as no other nation ever has been, the dread of tyrants and the hope of the friends of freedom. There have been Republics before: some have fallen, and some yet remain; but when the American Republic came into being, mankind felt that there was something peculiar in it: felt that a new element had come into human history; an element, which a deep and widespread presentiment seemed to tell them, would, sooner or later, work a vast change in the whole substance of that history.

Possibly someone may suggest, that if the Revolution were a necessity, then the causes which led to it were also a necessity: thus freeing from all blame the restrictive and tyrannous policy of the Mother Country towards the Colonies. Does any one think this? I answer that if that policy was blameless, then all unjust government is blameless; then all forms of sin are innocent; then the crucifiers of our Lord were not culpable;—but the case of the latter, as being innocent or blameworthy, has been settled by the inspired words of Peter. "*Him being delivered by the determinate counsel and foreknowledge of God, ye have taken and with wicked hands have crucified and slain.*"

There are no principles so operating in the Divine Government: there are no forces so working in human history, as to absolve either individuals or nations from the responsibility of their acts. Though we thus speak, we speak from no antipathy against our British parent; for we entertain for her feelings of filial regard.

Standing now on these principles, I see, if I mistake not, the hand of God most palpably apparent, working through the human agencies of the American Revolution. I see it in providing the means of incitement to meet the crisis. What were these? And where were they found? Whatever may be the feeling in the hearts of a people, all popular movements need direction: all popular enthusiasm needs expression. There is at such times a demand for minds able to conceive its sentiments, and tongues eloquent to put forth its utterances, stirring, through their electric words, still more profoundly the depths of the popular heart.

How was it, then, in our Revolutionary History in respect to this need? Divine Providence did not leave this want unmet; and it was never better met. It was met in such men as James Otis and Patrick Henry, the impassioned and triumphant defenders of popular Rights, and emphatically the orators of incitement to the Revolution, stirring and nerving the people to brave the crisis of offered resistance to tyranny. It was met in Samuel Adams and John Hancock, who, by the British authorities were declared to be outlaws. It was met in the Press, which sent forth its summons, conjuring the people to rise and battle for their rights. It was met in the Pulpit of the Revolution, which also uttered its voice; and its words resounded like a clarion blast throughout the land. It was met in the mothers, wives and sisters of the Revolution; for there were brave women in those days. Such were some of the men, for there were others of imperishable memory; and such were some of the influences in which were found the means of incitement to the struggle which won our National Independence.

The crisis was now at hand. In February, 1775, Parliament passed an Act, declaring that a rebellion existed in Massachusetts, and *"that an additional force should be sent to Boston."* Measures were hurried forward accordingly. With rash precipitancy, the authorities send a body of troops to seize on some military stores deposited at Concord. In the attempt to affect this, occurs the bloody tragedy at Lexington, and the war of the Revolution is already begun. Ethan Allen's magic capture of Ticonderoga, and the unresisting surrender of Crown Point two days afterward, inspirit the hearts and fix the determination of the patriots.

It is now time to inquire what means of accomplishing the work already begun by our fathers, did Divine Providence furnish. On the very day of Allen's capture of Ticonderoga, the Continental Congress commenced its second session at Philadelphia. One of the first objects of attention must, of course, be the appointment of a Commander-in-chief of the American forces. After a powerful speech, setting forth the qualities required in such a leader, John Adams concluded by nominating a man of their own body— "*George Washington, of Virginia.*" The House were electrified, and none more so than the individual on whom all eyes were so suddenly turned. The next day he was elected. Self-distrustingly, though manfully, he obeyed his country's call; and that country knows, and all the world knows, how well he justified those two days' transactions of Congress. Endowed from his birth with a well-formed and athletic frame, with a virtuous and noble character, with a high and fiery spirit, yet with matchless self-control, Divine Providence had, for years, been giving him special training for his work, while "*surveying wild lands and running boundary lines in the woods of Virginia,*" and by the part which he was required to perform in the French and Indian war. I cannot but think that the hand of God was signally manifest, and in nothing more so than in giving us just such a man as our Washington; so calm, so just, so firm, so wise to achieve our Independence; a second Moses to lead our American tribes from the Egypt of Colonial bondage through the Red Sea and wilderness of the Revolutionary struggle, to the Canaan of liberty. It is not too much to say that, had he been a different man, in the slightest essential degree, with his slender and precarious resources, with powerful enemies to encounter, with secret plottings for his deposition from office on the part of ambitious and unworthy men desirous of his place, with his unpaid, half-starved, ill-clad and shoeless soldiery, and worse than all, with Toryism and desertion rampant on all sides, he would have failed, for he would doubtless have ventured his little all on some rash hazard, and the American cause would have been lost. We sometimes hear him unfavorably compared, in a military point of view, with Eugene, or Marlborough, or Napoleon, or Wellington, or some other great Commander; but I must think that such comparisons proceed from a total misconception of his character.

Washington, in an emphatic sense, was a historical man; by that, I mean that he was a man prepared by Providence for a special end; called to perform a particular work, a work allowing him to be nothing other than just what he was. His destiny was not to dazzle or awe the world by august military achievements, sending down his name to the latest generations of men as a resistless conqueror, who might lead, like an Alexander or a Caesar, in proud triumph at his chariot wheels, the captive Chieftains of subjugated nations, because, for such an end he must have had at his command their disciplined and embattled cohorts; but it was to gain one simple, yet stupendous object, an achievement, in respect to its influence on the future of mankind, the most momentous in history; it was, with the scanty resources furnished to his hands, and with fearful odds against him, to lay the foundations of this great American Republic. Washington was a man so exactly fitted for his work, that, being changed at all, he would have been unequal to his task. Whether he himself recognized a Divine Providence as working in our American affairs; whether he regarded his country's cause as dependent upon that Providence, he would have told you, had you asked him on his coining from his knees in the forest seclusion, where he was accustomed to bow in prayer, while passing that dark winter at Valley Forge. I confess I have often been astonished that the spirit of the man did not break down; that the internal supports of his hope, courage and patriotism did not give way. The more I have studied American history, the more I have become convinced that, even with those who read the story of the Revolution, there is but a faint appreciation of the difficulties by which our Leader was surrounded. His spirit must have sunk within him before the close of seven long years, but for a twofold cause: and that was the firm hold which he had upon -first and highest principles, and the confidence which he felt in God as their supporter.

I must now proceed to say, that the same Providence which gave us Washington, gave us others also, who were worthy to be his brothers, if not his peers in the common cause of the country; but whose heroic deeds we have not time to record. It gave us Warren and Ward, Schuyler and Putnam, Gates and Montgomery, with others their compeers in the service and remembrances of a grateful country. It gave us, too, the sympathy of many minds of Continental Europe, and of not a few even in England. It called to our aid a Lafayette, a Steuben, a Kosciusco, with other Europeans, whose memories the country will embalm in a deathless gratitude. It gave us also one more, who has not received the recognition which his merit deserves, and whom we would not fail to mention here, I mean Robert Morris, the Financier of the Revolution, who rendered services, which, in their different form, were hardly less needful to the success of the cause than those of Washington himself, who, when money was indispensable, and when the country had no credit on which to raise money, could raise it on his own. This field, however, so rich in materials for illustrating our theme, the lack of time obliges me to leave.

Chapter Four

4. We recognize still another department of the illustration of God's peculiar Providential dealing with our people, in the constitutional period of our history.

Up to this era, God had conducted our fathers, illustrating our annals, at some points, by His marked interpositions, and, at all points, by obvious evidences of His peculiar care. To say nothing of the Trans-Atlantic preparations for our history, God had been with the Pilgrims from the hour when they first struck foot on Plymouth rock, to that which witnessed the recognition of our National Independence. Had He forsaken them then, ill would it have fared with our infant Republic.

To discuss the interior principles of the Constitution, to explain the structure of our Government, to trace the line of its practical workings, and to compare it with other systems form no part of my design. My purpose is simply to verify, by a few brief references, the presence of God's hand, working in this later, as I cannot but think I have done, in the earlier stages of our history.

The struggles of the Revolution past; the boon of Independence won; a new epoch was to be entered upon, and it was one of vast moment. Failing here, all that had gone before would go for nothing. First of all, at the critical moment of the close of the Revolution, God had already provided for the security of the country in the matchless character of Washington; had he not so done, this Government would have been a Monarchy, and not a Republic. This is the sublimest moment in the life of the great patriot. Having fought her battles, he is now seen laying down his honors at his country's feet; and, nobler than a Cincinatus, retiring to his home, when haply, like the Napoleons, he might have placed upon his brow, a crown. This was a solemn hour in the history of the country. The American cause needed men of far-sighted sagacity, of regulative talent, of constitutive ideas, of able statesmanship. It needed men of diplomatic abilities, those who would be faithful at home, and just abroad. It needed men of incorruptible patriotism, those who would till the offices of Government, not in the interest of self, but in that of the country. How adequately God supplied the men to meet these demands, our constitutional history leaves us in no doubt.

Certain Articles of Confederation, thirteen in number, adopted in November, 1777, had formed, during the course of the war, all the Constitution of Government that was requisite. The war being closed, the new condition of the country demanded a greater centralization of power, and a more efficient mode of Governmental action. The old Articles of Confederation found inadequate, were thrown aside, and our present Constitution, originally framed by Governor Morris, was submitted, in Sept. 1787, to the Continental Congress; copies of it were sent to the several States for ratification. How now was this Instrument received? Coming in conflict with extreme doctrines of State Sovereignty, it was violently opposed. Then were needed minds who could vindicate and support it; nor were they wanting; the men to meet this crisis were Madison, Hamilton and Jay. The result of their efforts was put forth in the Federalist, consisting of a series of political Papers, so fundamental in their principles, so clear in their reasonings, so masterly in their whole conception that European Statesmen have acknowledged their extraordinary value. To these remarkable writings the country is indebted, under God, in no small degree, for the ratification, by the several States, of the Constitution. The Constitution ratified, the offices of the Executive were to be filled, and the men, adapted to fill them, were not lacking, as the first Constitutional Cabinet will show. The national credit was sunk to its lowest depths, borne down by the mill-stone of a ponderous debt; Alexander Hamilton was called to the task of raising it, and he raised it.

A National Judiciary was to be established, and that clearheaded jurist, John Jay, came to the Bench as the first Chief Justice. Our nascent Republic had been, and was to be, represented in European Courts; and there were such men as Franklin, Jefferson, Pinckney, Livingston and Adams, with others of like character and fame to do it. While we may not affirm that demagoguism has had no place in our national affairs, for we know that it has; while we may not say that political corruption has never appeared in the tactics of partyism, for we know to the contrary; yet our American Congress has never been left without men, whose abilities have dignified its councils, and whose patriotism has made them watchful, that the Republic should receive no harm. History has recorded their names, and the country needs not the recital of them. These men, furnished by Providence, have gone forward devising, constituting and arranging, until they have produced for us the institutions, social, civil and political, which the God of our fathers, by means of them has handed down to us; and which, by us, and by those who shall come after us, may He convey to the most distant generations of posterity.

Such are some of the manifestations of God's hand in American history. Thus is our nation's awry full of passages telling of the marked and peculiar manner in which that hand has wrought in the various stages of our national progress. It is no Minerva planting her olives in our virgin soil; it is no Neptune, striking his trident into the rock of an American Acropolis; it is no Aeneas, escaping from a burning Troy, weathering the dire disasters sent by an angry Goddess, and setting, at last, his weary foot on these western shores; it is none of these, nor such as these, who may be honored as the founder of our glorious Republic. The genius of our country emerges not from the obscurity of misty legend; our history begins not in the wonders of lying fable, but its sources are found in God; and it is in the channels and under the guidance of His Providence, that, thus far, the stream of that history has flowed. There is, in this, no national vanity, seeking to dignify its annals, by claiming an illustrious origin; it is a truthful, a grateful, a religions, and an indispensable recognition.

To what other nation has God given such a history? To none. Then are we adequately conscious of, and adequately grateful for, the signal distinction which has been vouchsafed to us? Do we appreciate the peculiarities of our past history and of our present condition? To learn the value of our advantages, we have only to compare our condition with that of any other people.

Other countries have lofty mountains and noble rivers, beautiful lakes, fertile fields and lovely landscapes, as well as we. They have too what we have not; they have antiquity; they have the places where the older history was transacted; where the infancy of the race was cradled; where Civilization, Art and Literature took their rise.

They have Athens and Rome, with all the localities and monuments of classic times. They have the Pyramids, the Sphinxes and the Statue of Memnon. They have Thebes and Memphis, the plains on which the Pharaohs looked; the river, on whose sedgy [grassy] banks an Egyptian damsel found the infant Moses; they have Babylon and Nineveh, and more still; they have Sinai and Calvary, Jerusalem and Bethlehem, the land once trod by the feet of the Savior and his Apostles.

They have all these things; but what else do they have. They have Despotism watching, checking, restraining and oppressing them on every side: despotism in the State, and despotism in the Church; these two despotisms propping up each other, and crushing the people. They have expensive Courts, with all the gewgaws, the flourish and the foolery of Royalty to maintain. They have not only the ruling personages themselves to sustain, but their relatives to an indefinite number, even "to the third and fourth generation," a class who do nothing, except to eat up the substance of the people, whom they look down upon as an order of beings lower than themselves. They have standing armies to support in order to keep themselves in subjection: they have, I mean the masses, what seems to me scarcely better than an utter helplessness, in respect to all the true prospects of this life. This is what they have in most other countries.

However hoary [aged] then may be their antiquity: however interesting their historical associations: however rich their collections of Art: while we do not disesteem these disadvantages, shall we not more highly prize, and as firmly as possible hold, the invaluable gifts which God, in the development of His purposes respecting us as a people, has bestowed upon us. Our rulers are the men of our own election; and when they displease us, we can depose them, or, at the expiration of their terms, we can elect others; and our religion is that of our own choice. The Institutions of Learning also, hand in hand with those of Liberty and Religion, are scattering their blessings, either more or less, over every hill and valley in our land, extending the advantages of Education even to the humblest.

We have no titled aristocracy, as they have almost everywhere in the old world, separating, by the mere accident of birth, the rich from the poor, the high from the low; but with the blessing of God upon industry and virtue, the lowliest son of poverty may rise to stations of the highest honor and usefulness. It is such results as these that, God's Providence working in our history, has wrought out for us. Fellow citizens, do we rightly understand and appreciate these our National advantages? Do we fully and seriously apprehend, too, our mission as a people? God has not given us a history so peculiar without having in it an end in view: without having assigned to us duties which we must perform, and without having marked out for us a destiny which we must fulfill. Our advantages, then, have been bestowed with reference to those duties, and that destiny. Our mission is to show the world, the whole world, and on the grandest scale, the capacity of the people—the masses of the people—for self-government; the compatibility and coexistence of freedom with order; for freedom is not lawlessness, but the exercise of the human faculties, according to the principles of right and justice. Our mission is to show that Christianity, with respect to its organic structure, is not to exist in the form of a State Church,— the State holding up the Church as the oak does the vine: it is to show a free State and a free Church.

Our mission is to exhibit the results of general Education upon a great and free people; to give to humanity scope and place for culture and progress, and to present to the world, in herself, a realization and example of that culture and progress. In a word, it is to give to the world the theory and practice of constitutional and religious Freedom. That such a mission is for the world a most momentous one: that every true American citizen will seek, by all the means in his power, to secure the unchecked, the unaltered, the progressive and the perpetual development of a history which has been so auspiciously advanced to its present stage, and which, in its unchanged progress, is essential to the fulfillment of that mission, I need not pause to show.

Chapter Five

II. I come now, in the second place, to consider the bearings of the subject thus far discussed, upon the present historical crisis of the country.

1. I have spoken of the historic preparations by Providence for our national Life: of our broad Land and compact Nationality: of the hand of God as traced in our subsequent career: of our constitutional organization, and of the objects and ends of our American Republic. The Colonial and Revolutionary struggles were now ended: the processes of the Federal organization were completed: a recognition by European and foreign Powers was gained, and a national credit was established. The nation had a being, and stood forth before the world. Those who had framed and organized it saw the work of their hands, and as they looked upon it, might have borrowed, without irreverence, the words of Deity at the close of Creation, and pronounced it, as in their view, *"very good."*

The Ship of State was launched; Washington was placed at the helm, and she spread her canvas upon the broad sea of the future. Still, however complete her model; however excellent her construction; however noble her bearing, there was one leak in the hull of the Republic; though we are happy to believe that it is the only serious one, which the most thorough overhauling has ever detected. There was one rotten timber in her keel, and that was Slavery; but yet, as without it there would be a lack of materials, it was wrought into the structure, though with much perplexity as to the way of laying it, and with some misgivings as to the result. Jefferson and Madison uttered words of warning. Still they hoped for the best: they hoped that instead of increasing, the danger would diminish. Time rolled on: but instead of its diminution and cessation there has been an augmentation and a strengthening of the evil. The Slave Power, instead of diminishing and disappearing, as the founders of the Republic anticipated, has expanded in every dimension of census, interest, opinion and impudence, till it has precipitated "upon the country the crisis of today. And now what is that crisis? That unsound and dangerous spot, always in the ship's hull, has opened in a mighty bilge, and is letting in upon us the turbid and disastrous waters of rebellion. A dozen, either more or less, of once loyal States are, today, in armed revolt against the Government of the Union, seeking, by fire and sword, its overthrow, and the establishment of Slavedom upon its ruins.

Nor have these rebels done their work secretly. They have not whispered treason merely in the private ears of a few accomplices and confidential conspirators; but they have uttered it in the streets of the Capital and the halls of Congress. They have not spoken it merely in secret, but they have declared it upon the house-top: they have not merely skulked about under cover of the night, but they have stalked abroad at noon-day : they have violated the most solemn oaths: they have declared the ordinances of revolt: they have stolen the Government's money: they have robbed its Arsenals: they have seized its Forts: they have attacked its soldiers and defenders: they have opened and are prosecuting civil war, with circumstances of unheard-of perfidy, atrocity and barbarism.

Now what do they intend in all this? It is to make slavery coextensive with the country: to remove its metes, bounds and hindrances: to give it unrestricted scope and enduring perpetuity; it is to gratify the ambition of a set of conscienceless demagogues, reared in the lap of oppression, who, when they can no longer rule, are determined to ruin: who, taking the people by the head have run them into the abyss of rebellion.

And what were the expectations with which the conspirators entered upon their work? They had the atrocious presumption, the measureless audacity to suppose that, with what strength they have of their own, and with what help would be supplied by northern treason, they could crush down all opposition: take the Government bodily, and reconstruct it on their own principles, looking to the vaults in Wall Street and State Street to pay the bills. And what are the means by which these men are seeking to accomplish their end? It is by lying, by theft, by murder, by conscription, by intensifying the hatred of the Southern people against the National Government, whose objects they designedly misrepresent. Such are the aims, the hopes and the means of this gigantic rebellion, with which the conspiracy of Cataline is not to be compared.

Was there nothing in the sacredness of our national history to challenge their reverential regard? Was there nothing in the signal dealings of God's Providence with us, as a nation, which we have already traced, and which stamp their inviolable seal upon our national character, to restrain them from such a mad and nefarious course? Was there nothing in the objects and ends as we have pointed them out, for which that Providence planned, and thus far has wrought out our history to be to them an influence and a motive of refrain? Was there nothing in the labors performed, in the sacrifices rendered, in the sufferings endured, in the blood spilt by the fathers, to arouse their patriotism? Was there nothing in the sanctity of old associations and the ties of national brotherhood to attach them to their country? Was there nothing in the echoes of Hanover Court House? Nothing from the graves of De Kalb and Pulaski? nothing in the shades of Monticello and Mount Vernon, to deter them from this atrocious conspiracy? Was there nothing in the memory of Eutaw Springs and the Cowpens? Nothing in the heroic deeds of Jasper, Moultrie and Sumter to prevent them from firing upon their country's flag, and cannonading the fort that bears the patriot's name? No. Nothing! Nothing! That priceless, that paramount interest of slavery is at stake; and all ties, all obligations, all principles, all interests are as nothing before it; are as ropes of sand and as flax in the fire.

Wesley pronounced slavery to be *"the sum of all villainies."* The definition is pungent and complete. We have always believed it true, but never so cordially, so deeply, so entirely as today. For slavery alone, its advocates and propagandists are ready to give up or destroy everything beside. For this one thing, and that the worst and most infernal of all things, since all sins and all wrongs, oppression, adultery, rebellion and murder, are potentially wrapped up with it, and reside within it; they are ready to sacrifice everything—their country's Government, its history, its hopes, its destiny, its glory, with the prospects and interests of freedom and religion for the world. For this one tiling, in a sacrament of blood and death, they pledge *"their lives, their fortunes,"* and would their *"sacred honor,"* if they had any to pledge. They are demolishing the southern wall of the Temple of Freedom, and with its fragments, they are attempting to lay the foundations of despotism. Against law, against duty, against precedent, against the sense of all mankind beside, they have inaugurated a Slave Confederacy on the soil won from tyranny by the toils and blood of the fathers, and consecrated to liberty. They have told the world that its Corner-stone is slavery; they need not have specified any particular part as being that thing, for slavery is the top, bottom and sides of the whole concern.

Thus there is an attempt to found, on southern soil, and in the very bosom of this American Republic, the Empire of slavery, while all the world beside is tending towards liberty; while Alexander, of Russia, is emancipating his serfs; while Joseph, of Austria, is promising constitutional guarantees to his Hungarian subjects; while Poland and Italy are striving for independent nationalities; while all Europe is looking towards freer Governments and freer Institutions.

Are we told, however, in apology for their iniquitous proceeding, that the social and political ideas of the age, will, in a short time, veer round to be upon their side; that, though the tendency toward freedom is just now the course of the world, in a decade it will turn back again to its old ruts? For six thousand years it has been turned toward despotism; now, that it is heading the other way, we think, that for a while, it will stay so headed.

Shall we be referred for another justification of their rebellion, to the exasperations which, it is alleged, that the South has received from the free-speaking and fanaticism of the North? It is true we have spoken with some freedom because we could not alter our consciences, because we could not prevent our thoughts, because we could not altogether repress them; but as for the fanaticism of the North, except in the case of the foray of John Brown, approved by almost nobody, it has been the spirit of absolute quiescence compared with the barbarous fanaticism of the South, whose weapons are not words, but cudgels and bowie knives, pistols and halters.

As for the Government, meanwhile, what has it not done to appease the Moloch of slavery? It has twisted and turned; it has bowed itself down; it has eaten dirt; it has done everything it could do, in reason and out of reason, to propitiate this great demon of the South. It has framed no Congressional bill, that has not been squared and adjusted to the demands and interests of slavery. It has given its offices and emoluments in disproportion to Southerners, who have been too proud and too lazy to work, and they have paid back the Government by treason and rebellion.

Where now are the justifications of this transcendent villainy? They are nowhere! A declaration of independence, setting forth the causes which have influenced them to this course, drawn up in the form of that drafted by our fathers, would be a note-worthy document to come before the world. *"The opinions of mankind"* would scout it from civilized society. Out of Cottondom there is not a throne of despotism on earth half wicked enough to put forth the sentiments which such a Manifesto would contain. Though without the shadow of a justification, they have, nevertheless, rushed onward to their dreadful work, which, if they are permitted to accomplish, will cut short, at once and forever, the course of American history.

Chapter Six

2. How now was the first scene in this bloody drama opened? The Government are essaying to supply with provisions, a handful of half-starved men in one of its own forts; that fort is assaulted and fired, and the American flag is struck to the ground. I believe that the end of the drama thus opened, God will take under his own control. I believe that, in this case, as always, the wrath of man shall praise Him, and any remainder, over and above what would subserve that end, I believe He will restrain. Be assured of this, that the same Providence, so many traces of which we find in all our country's past, is presiding also over the events of this stormy hour. The God of our history permits, indeed, this work to go on; but know of a truth, He does not permit it without an object in view.

I believe that one intent of the permission is, to make the insane fury of the perpetrators of this horrid wrong, the means of their own punishment, thereby to instruct mankind, in a great principle of God's Providential discipline of nations. In such a plan, He is only repeating a course which he has not infrequently pursued in the history of States. Thus was it in the case of the Egyptians, whom God submerged in the Red Sea. For a long time the southern people have been strengthening the fetters of oppression; for a long time they have been forming themselves to a semi-barbarian type of character, carrying habitually with them weapons of death, and ready, at the slightest misunderstanding or affront, to get up a duel. For a long time, the slaveholder has been wont to despise our Northern people, most of whom Divine Providence has obliged to work for a living, while he takes his out of the labor of slaves,—forcibly, if not voluntarily rendered, and paid only as a man pays his horse, by giving him food and shelter that he may not become unable to work. They have opprobriously [shameful, disgraceful] spoken of us as forming the "mudsills" of society: perhaps we do; but if so, they form its cockloft [small loft, attic]; and we submit, whether it looks well for the cockloft of society to boast itself so over the mudsills!

These obnoxious ideas, these offensive taunts, and the form of character that is the source from which they spring, are the baleful and inevitable result of the unnatural, 'wicked and corrupting constitution of society among them. Is the Lord going to suffer such pride, such oppression, such guilt, such madness, as are now theirs, to escape unpunished? It is worse than idle to expect it. We may not close our eyes to the teachings of God's Providence in History, which are the same with those of His Word. Surely He will make their own wicked rage and demented foolhardiness, if they persevere in the attempt to sunder the Republic, the means of their chastisement, if not of their destruction. It is to be hoped that through this fearful judgment, which by their folly and sin they have pulled down upon their own heads, they will *"learn righteousness;"* but however this may be, there can be no doubt that God intends, by means of this awful condition into which their own guilty conduct has plunged them, that at least the inhabitants of the world shall *"learn righteousness."*

He will teach the nations the doom of oppressors, which, by their stolidity, by their rashness, by their infatuation, they prepare for themselves. He will teach them a lesson which history illustrates, but which they are prone to forget, that there is a stage, sometimes reached, in the career of the oppressor, in which, besotted by his fatuity, and drunk with the wine of his madness, he prepares his own winding-sheet, digs his own grave, plunges into it; and mankind have only to close his funeral by heaping upon him the dirt of disgrace, contempt and abhorrence, which his deeds of darkness have merited.

If we mistake not, by this awful crisis in our nation's history, Divine Providence would teach us, too some lessons. With our immense expansion, with the rapid increase of wealth, the great mass of our people have grown intensely sordid and material in character ; amassing money, or trying to amass it, only to hoard it up with a miserly closefistedness, or to expend it in a proud, profligate and luxurious extravagance, hardly recognizing, unless it is by virtual compulsion, that there are any objects in the philanthropic, the intellectual, the moral and the religious interests of the world, for which property is given, and to which it must be applied.

In the awful exigency which has come upon us, God has broken into the safes of this iron selfishness: He has untied a million purse-strings, not only the loosely-drawn, but the hard-knotted, by showing the people that there are interests more valuable than money: more valuable than even individual life. The patriotic patience with which multitudes of business men have suffered and are suffering intense, and even ruinous pecuniary pressure, coming down unrepiningly from affluence to penury, is a phenomenon of this great crisis, to me hardly less impressive than the readiness with which thousands have rushed to arms, periling [endangering] their lives for the rescue of their country. God would show our people that great principles can be maintained only at the cost of great sacrifices. He, himself has made them; so must we. In these days of official theft, of wholesale defalcations, of general time-serving, the support of principle by sacrifice has with many almost died out from the small crop of even their traditional virtues. To a great extent our people are living as though this life is everything; and duty, principle, eternity nothing. By this great crisis in our history may God teach us a different lesson.

Nor is this all: if my judgment does not mislead me, He would show us likewise some of the ripe fruit of the doctrines of latitudinarianism and non-coercion, so widely sown within a few years past; and which are rapidly going to seed in almost every department of our moral life, in a weakened and vitiated sense of the sanctions of duty. The basis of a deep, strong and noble character, whether individual or national, is never laid, except under the regimen of a wholesome moral discipline. Parents who are bringing up untrained offspring are heaping together the firebrands of Revolution; and that Government which is feebly administered with respect to the treatment of crime, is destined to fall to pieces, relaxing at every joint through sheer corruption. Such a Government may be progressive; but it is down a steep hill to its own destruction: it is going where Greece and Rome went, and by the same road. Then may this crisis be the means of reinstating that principle which, in our people, has become dangerously unsettled, but which is the foundation of all high and sound character—loyalty to law, human and Divine. Let this be, and all shall be well. Let the country be true to herself, and true to her glorious history, in all that it involves for the good of humanity and the glory of God; let her give all traitors and rebels to understand, that she has for them but a few very simple articles, namely, bullets and bayonets, ropes and gibbets, for the magistrate may not bear the sword in vain, then will there be hereafter for that class of citizens but slender encouragement; then will the Government come forth from the struggle purer and stronger, both in itself and in view of the world, than before the experience of this fiery probation.

What now, I ask, shall we do? The hour is a solemn one—the most momentous in the country's history. Asking God, on whom we depend, in the language of Dr. Wayland, *"to issue this awful exigency in the glory of His Son;"* entreating Him to give to all our citizens virtue and patriotism, and especially to our rulers and legislators wisdom to know their duty, and courage to do it; and thanking Him meanwhile for the wonderful degree of these great qualities already exhibited by them, what, I again ask, shall we do? Shall we give up our national history, and look upon its last chapter as ending here? Shall we contemplate the hand of God as working in such a wonderful manner in our historical career, only to close up, in an abrupt collapse, a violent frustration of all its apparent plans and purposes? Shall this greatest and best realization of Republican Freedom which the world has ever seen, be ruthlessly destroyed? Shall we disappoint the expectation of myriads who are suffering under oppression, and who are looking to our shores for the great hope and true home of down-trodden Liberty in all lands? Patriotism, Freedom and Religion answer No! Shall we sleep in torpid supineness until we are awakened by the iron heel of the despot upon our necks? Shall we permit the slave master to call his sable menials under the shadow of Bunker Hill Monument, as he has said that he will do? The true sons of sires who served their country on Bemis' and Bunker's heights, on Erie and Champlain, answer No! The heroes of Lundy's Lane and Fort Sumter, answer No! What! shall that traitorous Palmetto flag, the vile emblem of Slavery, (ever float over the Granite hills and the Green Mountains of New England: on the banks of the Hudson, and from the summits of the Adirondacks? Shall it be raised in the Metropolis of the Empire State, and surmount the Keystone of the Federal Arch? Shall it be unfurled on the breezy prairies of the Northwest, and by the leaping waters of Niagara? No! An echo starting from the headlands of Maine, reverberated across a Continent and dying away on the waves of the Pacific, answers No! The flag of the

Union shall ever, as now, wave over them all; and not only so, but the National Motto shall be *"the Stars and Stripes on every flag-staff from Maine to Texas."*

Do these men, however, begin to show signs of readiness to retreat from their purpose of Northern subjugation? Do they not tell us that they only want to be *"let alone?"* Do they not know that the thief, the adulterer, the highwayman, and the murderer, only want the same thing? Do they not know that the *"let-alone"* doctrine is specially held at Charlestown, Sing-Sing, Auburn and Dannemora? What! are they to be allowed to break up this Government? Are they to be allowed to terminate the line of American history? If so, then having in our hands the means to prevent it, we are, with respect to our allegiance to God, as well as the spirit, the principles and ends of our History, blacker traitors than they. If this Government is overthrown or rent in twain, then the hopes of the world for popular Institutions are at an end. The boding auguries of European Absolutists are fulfilled. We number ourselves with Mexico and the wretched States of Central and South America, whose very name is a by-word, a reproach and a poison to Freedom.

Must we be told, however, that the Theory of our Government so differs from that of absolute ones, that the rebels must be treated in a correspondingly different manner? in other words, that coercion cannot be applied. Governments may fail practically, as they not infrequently have failed; but where before has there ever been a Government which had the principle of its destruction, systematically wrought into its very theory? Nowhere. Must we hear more, too, of the doctrine of *"peaceable secession,"** as for months it has been put forth from tongue and pen, demoralizing the public conscience, and blinding it to the turpitude of this atrocious rebellion. It is the greatest political heresy that was ever promulgated, for if on this principle the country may be divided into halves, then on the same principle it may be divided into much smaller factions.

(* See the address delivered by the Hon. Edward Everett in New York, July 4th, 1861 in which the whole question is treated in a manner which elsewhere we have not seen equaled.)

Or again, is a vile compromise to be made with the Government by the rebels,—they coming to offer its self-dictated terms with one hand, while the weapons of threatened revolt and destruction are in the other? No; let them lay down their rebel arms, and become again loyal citizens, before they venture into the presence of their injured country. Let them do this, or let the country go steadily onward to their subjugation. Otherwise let us not hereafter speak of the American Government, unless it be as recalling with sadness the story of what it once was; for it exists no longer. It has sunk out of history into the mire of a fathomless debasement: it has perished in the void of absolute nothingness; and that vile thing culling itself Government, which remains in its place, I will pray for power to loathe more and more as long as I breathe this vital air. Troy was; but is no longer.

The hopes of the millions, of other continents, struggling for freedom—civil, political and religious—and looking to this land to behold the prospects and read the promises of the future, are stricken from the earth. Long have despots tried to prove that popular Governments are no Governments. They never doubted that the American Republic is strong enough for external purposes; the question has ever been and is, whether it will prove itself adequate to internal ones. Let the Government compromise with armed rebels, and the question is settled. A hundred fold better would it be, with respect to the interests of freedom, that the country should go into this struggle and fail, if such an event were possible, than that it should shrink from meeting the crisis; European powers would have for us, in the former case, a remaining respect, for they have had similar experiences; but in the latter, none.

Why, however, do we add argument to argument? Looking once for all to the historical Homestead of this great people, nothing can be plainer, than that it never was intended for two hostile nations: before it can be thus occupied, God must reconstruct the continent, cutting to the ocean, as an outlet for the great Northwest, a river running on Mason's and Dixon's line.

Then let the country stand firm. Let all her citizens see the question as standing heaven-high above all mere party issues: let all patriots, the lovers of Freedom and the lovers of their race surround her standard, and whether they come from the field or the shop, from the marts of Commerce, the halls of Science, or the Sanctuaries of Religion; let them maintain her cause. And do thou, O! God of our Fathers, if it may be, bring these men to a better mind and a better purpose, that they may restore their allegiance to Thyself, and to this most beneficent of human Governments; but if it may not be, that they will lay down their bloody arms, and come into the line of Thy great purposes of History, regarding Thy glory, and the good of mankind, through this once happy people, then do Thou, blast with the breath of Thy nostrils, their infernal designs, scattering them to the winds of Heaven; and let the curse of Meroz, scathing with the fires of Perdition, fall upon that man, or that class of men, whoever they may be, whether from the South or the North, from the East or the West, who shall lift the hand for the overthrow, or the rupture of this God-founded Republic.

Book Three
GOD'S HAND IN AMERICA

By: The Rev. George B. Cheever

With An Essay,
By The Rev. Dr. Skinner.

*Change wide, and deep, and silently performed,
This Land shall witness; and, as days roll on,
Earth's universal frame shall feel the effect,
Even till the smallest habitable rock,
Beaten by lonely billows, hear the songs
Of Christianized society, and bloom
With civil arts, and send their fragrance forth,
A grateful tribute to all-ruling Heaven.
The Excursion. (Book IX)*

Essay 77
Introduction 84

Part One
A Governing and Retributive Providence Among the Nations

CHAPTER 1: God The Governor Among The Nations.-Universal Disregard Of This Truth 86

CHAPTER 2: Principles Of God's Dealings With The Nations 90

CHAPTER 3: Nature And Execution Of The Divine Retributive Providences 93

CHAPTER 4: Elements Of National Gratitude And Responsibility, The Word Of God, The Christian Sabbath, A Converted Ministry, The Holy Spirit. A Good Government, Freedom Of Opinion, Common Schools 101

PART 2
Indications Of The Divine Providence Concerning The Destiny And Duty Of The United States

CHAPTER 5: Particulars Op The Divine Providence, Our Origin, Our Government, Our Previous And Successive Discipline, Freedom From A Religious Establishment 109

CHAPTER 6: Particulars Of The Divine Providence Continued, A Regenerated And Educated Ministry, Revivals Of Religion, Prevalence Of The English Language 117

CHAPTER 7: Enumeration Continued, Rapid Increase Of Our Population, Our Common School Education, Our Relative Geographical Position... 121

CHAPTER 8: Designs Of God In Our Discipline, And The Blessedness Of Their Fulfillment On Our Part 126

CHAPTER 9: Interest And Grandeur Of The Divine Experiment With Us As A People, Conditions Of Success, Causes At Work To Disturb And Thwart It 132

CHAPTER 10: Lessons Of Individual Responsibility And Duty, A High Standard Of Piety, A Holy Education, The Right Use Of Property, The Right Use Of Prayer, Conclusion 136

ESSAY

It has been groundlessly objected to the Ethics of Christianity, that they deny Patriotism a place among the virtues. Although there is no specific inculcation of this sentiment in the New Testament, it should not be hence inferred that the Gospel either disowns or underrates it, as one of the modifications of that love which is the fulfilling of the law. The Jews were now in a state of vassalage to Rome, and appeals to the love of country, in their circumstances, would have been understood by them as a summons to rebellion against the established government; and had Christianity made such appeals, it would have taught disobedience to one of its sternest precepts,—that which demands submission to the civil authorities. Again; this unhappy people were, at this time, the subjects of a fanaticism which made malignity towards other nations a duty in their eyes, and addresses to patriotism would, in their case, have been, in effect, only supplying fuel to the fire of an already rancorous hatred of mankind.

But more than all, this disobedient and gainsaying nation, whose history from the beginning had been little else than a record of abuses of miraculous mercy, had only to perpetrate the murder of Christ, in order to fill the measure of their guilt, and bring on themselves those unexampled visitations of the Divine wrath, by which their political existence was destroyed; and our blessed Savior, who was well aware of the gathering of the storm, and of the desolation it would produce, was too deeply moved with compassion, to be instilling lessons of patriotism into their breasts, while everything in their condition demanded alarms and calls to repentance.

The time, moreover, had arrived when the dispensation of Liberty was about to supersede that of Restraint, and all nations, in respect of religious privileges, to be placed on the same level. The middle wall of separation between Jews and Gentiles was in the process of demolition, and exhortations to the love of country, either in the one or the other, would have had no other tendency than to engender mutual antipathies, and thus prevent the accomplishment of the gracious design.

But the silence of Christianity on that topic, at such a time, no more implied either hostility or indifference to patriotism, universally and absolutely, than our silence as to the sin of intemperance, on a sacramental occasion, supposes us indifferent to the guilt and ravages of that sin.

The Gospel indeed proclaims peace and good will to the world; it seeks to make all men, in reference to earth, pilgrims and strangers, to unite them in one holy and happy brotherhood, and to subject them to new and celestial relationships strong and lasting as eternity, and embracing, in their wide scope, the entire universe of the virtuous and the good, both on earth and in heaven. But the reasoning which would hence infer any inconsistency in the spirit of the Gospel with the highest degrees of devotion to the welfare of our country, would make Christianity subversive of the foundations of society; and opposed not to nationality only, but to the continuance of the human race. For if the love of country be excluded by the predominance of that heavenly-mindedness which the Gospel inculcates, so are the love of neighborhood, and the love of domestic relatives, and all the endearments of friendship, and all local attachments, and the pursuits of business, and labors for a household provision, and whatever else is necessary to the continued existence of man in this world.

It is admitted that Philanthropy, and not patriotism, is the comprehensive expression of the spirit of the Gospel, in reference to mankind. But there may be expansion without inconsistence; and there may be limitations and degrees, and various forms of interest and affection, along with the most perfect harmony and unity of spirit. A philanthropy which has no particular localities, no definite spheres of labor, no fixedness of regards, no specific tasks, no preferences, no individual or vicinal trials and pleasures, is a mere abstraction: why then may not the love of country consist with, nay be a genuine modification of the love of man? Nothing is more manifest, than that the same law of nature, which unites us, in different degrees of affection, with different portions and individuals of our kind, must originate a peculiar love of country, in every unperverted, undebased heart; and therefore to make the spirit of Christianity opposed to patriotism, is to make it unnatural.

There is a species of patriotism, so called, which the Gospel does not approve. It was the maxim of Themistocles, that whatever is advantageous to one's country is just; but as that self-love is criminal which pursues its purpose in violation of another's rights, so is that love of country, if it must be so termed, which wantonly interferes with the peace and independence of other nations. Christianity has no encouragement for the darings, no sympathy with the spirit, of an Alexander or a Napoleon, or of any one of the great conquerors, whose exploits history has recorded or poetry sung. On the contrary, language has no terms of reprobation, strong enough to express its hostility to all, whether individuals or nations, who trench on the peace and liberty and inalienable rights of others, to aggrandize themselves. A plundering army is, in the sight of God, but an association of robbers and murderers, whose individual retributions, will be neither stayed nor alleviated, in the Day of Judgment, because they were banded together and headed by a brave and skilful chief. The triumphs of the Roman generals, which filled the imperial city with exultation, moved Heaven with purposes of exterminating wrath against the nation.

The religion of Christ, is also opposed to the vaunted patriotism of the spirit of party. The Gospel obliges us to seek the country's good; not the success of one portion of the community, in opposition to another. It may be, that the interests of the party and of the country, are identical; in which case, while Christianity requires us to pursue those interests, it forbids our doing so with the feelings of rivalry; and, if we disregard the prohibition, however successful we may be, it denies us the praise of love to the nation. Good may come to the country by our means, but our condemnation will be just, unless an honest zeal for the nation's happiness, not the party's triumph, be the motive of our conduct.

It has been questioned whether Christians, and especially ministers of the Gospel should not stand aloof from all political contests, and either not vote at elections, or conceal their votes, so that their preference among rival candidates for office shall not be known. But it is a purely selfish and time-serving prudence which ordinarily suggests this course. There may be rare occasions, when reserve and even inaction may be demanded; and our moderation and equanimity should always be exemplary; but the cause of our country is in all respects too important, and especially too closely connected with the interests of religion, to permit anyone who is controlled by principle and the spirit of the Gospel, to be, in common cases, either negative or unknown, in the influence which he exerts. Shall the interests of the nation be abandoned to the blind and headlong action of partisan zeal? Where the State, as with us, deprives no man of the elective franchise, no man should deprive himself of it; and if public sentiment is any where opposed to a clergyman in the calm and regular exercise of this privilege, he ought therein to be opposed to public sentiment; showing that he loves his country and his Savior too well, and is too sensible of his final responsibility to God, to consent to the perpetual disuse of any talent, which has been put into his hands.

A patriotism, governed in its exercises by the precepts of the Gospel, cannot be revolutionary, so long as government is administered according to legitimate authority or the commission granted by the laws. We may have, and frankly express, our opinions of cabinet measures and legislative enactments. Under our responsibility to God, we should examine, and judge whether the executive head of the nation, and all subordinate officers, act in their respective stations, with or without authority; and if the limits of power are transgressed by them, we are not bound either to silence or to passive submission. A peculiarity of circumstances may render resistance unavailing, and therefore inexpedient; but to maintain that non-resistance is universally our duty in such cases, is to place God on the side of absolute tyranny, and to deny the permanent obligation of patriotism, unless it be the invariable fact, that the interest of the country demands that magistrates, do what they may, should be left unmolested. But so long as the government which is administered is that which has been established, and so long as the administration is constitutional and regular, however imperfect in other respects, the spirit and proceedings of true patriotism will be anti-revolutionary; and while it may regret and censure freely, the want of wisdom, firmness, clemency, and principle, in the powers that be, will not only obey, but sustain, if need be with arms, those duly constituted powers, against all rival ones, foreign or domestic; and this it will do from regard at once to the country's welfare and the will of God, who has declared the established authorities to be his own ministers, and those who resist them to be adversaries to his ordinance.

It is said that Christianity forbids the use of arms, and every form of war, and thus makes martial courage, if not patriotism a sin. But though the Gospel would beat swords into ploughshares, and spears into pruning-hooks, and fill the world with love and peace and joy, and though it employs a tone and emphasis of teaching against wars and fightings, which makes the responsibility for them dreadful, yet it gives no ground for the conclusion, that it is unchristian or unlawful to serve one's country in the camp or on the field of battle. When we consider what is written concerning the four centurions; and the advice of John the Baptist to the soldiers; and that the principle which so expounds the scriptures in question, as to draw from them testimony against arms, has not its limit in that inference, but equally condemns all punishments of crime, and either takes the sword from the magistrate, or makes him bear it in vain, if it does not render government itself a crime,—we find ourselves obliged to protest against this interpretation of the Gospel, as in the highest degree rash, fanatical and injurious. Great as are the horrors of war, the same principle which vindicates the Divine Government, in permitting these and infinitely greater evils, namely, that the highest good of the whole must be maintained against all opposers, at whatever hazards or consequences,—vindicates and demands the use of weapons of war in support of the government of the country, legitimately administered, against all assailants from without or from within.

The spirit of true patriotism is one with the spirit of all just government in seeking as its last end, not the good of the rulers but the ruled. And because this is not to be identified with increase in numbers, or territory, or wealth, or magnificence, but with intelligence and virtue, the only ground of solid and permanent happiness; and because these are to be secured in their highest measures only by the prevalence of religion, through the land, therefore, while an enlightened love of country must zealously promote the cause of popular education, it must be mainly intent on the evangelization and conversion of all the inhabitants. They unquestionably are the nation's best friends, who by holy living, and missionary labors and sacrifices, are infusing the leaven of the Gospel into the mass of the population. In this country, the State cannot use the public treasure in advancing Christianity, but that every statesman and ruler, and judge, should be a Christian in all his conduct, private and official, and should particularly be a zealous and liberal patron of Home missions, is demanded alike by patriotism and by religion. One of the greatest duties that we owe to our country, is Prayer for those who are in authority over it. If they are wise and holy men, they certainly have a claim on the nation's prayers, and much more if they are not. It is a good thing among the English, though their enforcing it by law is not good, that their established Church never performs the divine service, without a distinct and solemn and supplicatory mention of the chief magistrate, and the legislature of the nation; and it is also a good and a patriotic thing, that the branch of the American Church which uses a liturgy, has obliged itself to do the same in respect to the civil authorities of this country.

If any Christian denomination be wanting in this particular, they are reproved by these examples. But it should content no one, in this high matter, to offer with others, ceremonious prayer, however solemnly and constantly. In the hands of those who hold the high places of magistracy, legislation and judgment, lie the springs of the national weal, and they cannot be touched without consequences of good or evil to every interest, civil and spiritual, throughout the whole land. There is not a village, nor a church, nor a family, nor an individual, whose interests are not committed to the country's head and council; and though the Christian's life be hid with Christ in God, and though the final triumph of the Church be certain, and though the country's purest and best men have the management of its affairs, yet it is only presumption to expect that the happiness of either country, church or Christian, is safe, if importunate and continual prayer be not offered on behalf of those who bear the responsibilities, burdens and temptations of government. The most earnest prayer for them is specifically and urgently demanded of every individual; and he is the true patriot who meets the demand.

Though the Church in this land be separate from the State, there is no power which can be brought into action in favor of the nation's happiness, equal to that of the Pulpit. The energies of this divine means of every good to man, are greatly increased with us, by its disconnection from all civil advantages and aids. If it receive no support, it is under no obligations but those of love. If it stand alone, yet it is independent and free; while there is no place near or remote, no person high or low, no subject-matter, whether of politics, legislation, morals, religion, science or art, to which it may not boldly apply its appropriate influence, under protection of the government, so long as it violates no one's civil rights. This privilege has the American pulpit:—its field is boundless, its way is unobstructed, it may make a full experiment of its powers, and if it does this, the proof to the country will be perfect, that the Gospel is the best friend to all human interests, national and individual, temporal as well as eternal; the State will reverence and cherish, though it cannot espouse the Church, and the peace of our rising and spreading republic will flow as a river, and its righteousness as the waves of the sea.

The volume, from which this essay has too long detained the reader, shows that its author is aware of the breadth of his proper sphere as a minister of Christ. He supposes himself empowered to treat other subjects besides those to which the assiduities of the pulpit are generally given. In his character as a clergyman, he has felt himself authorized, to address his fellow citizens, as in the pages of this book, on relations and responsibilities of infinite moment, involving every interest of their own and their posterity. And while he has endeavored to enlarge their view of the ulterior influence of the country, on the welfare of the world, he has added new and overpowering force to every other motive to the discharge of all individual and national obligations.

We owe the author our thanks for thus directing our attention to God's Hand In America. That Hand has been progressively revealing itself from our commencement as a people, until at length in vivid distinctness, and in great power of instruction, admonition and promise, it is lifted high before the eyes of the world. In the operations of Providence, no man can fully understand the beginning till the end is known. It has been profoundly remarked, that as there is nothing in the universe, not even the minutest atom which floats in the sunbeam, nor the dewdrop which covers the most secret flower, that stands alone, but all blends with all; so individual existence and individual phenomena can only be explained by explaining the whole. The progress and connections of things however, discover with increasing light, that the divine agency in them is ever directed by reference to a definite purpose and a settled plan; and *"men of wisdom"* perceive with the liveliest interest the traces of design as they gradually unfold themselves, and like the angels, have a holy desire to know as much as possible before-hand, concerning the final result. This country is yet in its early youth, but the steps of Providence toward it have been so remarkable, that it stands in the world almost as a finished monument of the divine power, and from the opposite shores of the Atlantic, *"the eyes of the oppressed are even now turning wistfully to the land of freedom, and the kings of the continent already regard with awe and disquietude the new Rome rising in the west, the foreshadows of whose greatness, yet to be, are extending dark and heavy over their dominions, and obscuring the luster of their thrones."*

Nevertheless, no principle of God's administration hath received more signal illustration from the past, than that privileges imply duties; and well does this book remind us that, *the Divine Being might make a short work upon the earth, and yet within its limits there might be traced the overthrow and destruction of a nation like our own, because of our ingratitude, and the selection and preparation of another people for the accomplishment of the Divine purposes of mercy to the world.* The Jews themselves had scarcely greater reason to fear that the vials of the wrath of God, would be emptied upon them if they should prove rebellious, than have the inhabitants of this land, if they fail to recognize and fulfill their peculiar obligations as the most favored of mankind.

Introduction

The bearing of the political and social relations of the world at the present moment upon the advancement of the Redeemer's kingdom, is atopic so fruitful in interest and instruction, that whatever thoughts, in a reverential spirit, may be thrown out upon it, can scarcely fail to find a welcome. The series of experiments and demonstrations in truth and error, of which this world has been for thousands of years so grand a theatre, there is some reason to believe is drawing towards its close, and is soon to be followed by the perfect reign of righteousness on earth. There appears to be an enlargement of the movements and indications of Divine Providence, from particulars to generals; and there is a concentration of interest upon our own country, looking a few years in advance of our present position, which invests the study of the principles of the divine conduct with the most absorbing importance.

A general view of the grounds of national responsibility and retributive providence may fitly precede a more particular examination of the divine providential dealings and indications towards us as a people. This current of thought the author has pursued in two discourses, delivered in the Allen-street church, the first on occasion of the day of public thanksgiving in this State, and the other on the first Sabbath evening in the year, the evening previous to the day of prayer for the world's conversion. The second discourse was also repeated in the Mercer-street church, in this city.

The substance of these discourses is now presented in a shape somewhat different, but adapted to exhibit more impressively and clearly the unity and importance of the theme. The general propositions traced in its first division may be enumerated as follows:

1. That God is governor among the nations.
2. That he deals with nations on the same principles as with Individuals.
3. That the responsibilities and duties of nations as individuals, are commensurate with their capabilities, opportunities, and mercies.
4. That the disregard and violation of this principle will be followed with the divine retribution, and if persisted in, must result in national degradation and ruin.
5. That in the light of these principles an enumeration of the elements of national gratitude, is an exceedingly solemn and admonitory service.

These propositions may occupy two or three of the following chapters, and afterwards the main subject to which they are introductory will be discussed, viz: The opportunities and responsibilities of this country for its own and the world's evangelization. Here opens that most striking aspect of providence and duty, to which I have referred in the general title of this volume; a title which may be pardoned for its apparent singularity and quaintness, in consideration of its condensed expression of a most comprehensive and important theme.

Part One
A Governing and Retributive Providence Among the Nations

> Vengeance will sit above our faults; but till
>   She there do sit,
> We see her not, nor them.
>   Thus blind, yet still
> We lead her way; and thus, whilst we do ill,
>   We suffer it. -- Donne.

Chapter 1
God The Governor Among The Nations, Universal Disregard Of This Truth

There are a few passages in Scripture where the rule of God's providence, and the mode of his dealings among the nations, are quite as explicitly revealed, as the precepts of the divine law in the Decalogue. Of this nature is that most remarkable passage in the 28th chapter of the prophecy of Jeremiah, of which the ninth and tenth verses constitute an important portion. Considered in connection with the 25th chapter of the same prophecy, and the illustration of it, on so vast and awful a scale, in the destruction of the Jewish people, it becomes exceedingly solemn. *At what instant I shall speak concerning a nation, and concerning a kingdom, to build and to plant it, if it do evil in my sight, that it obey not my voice, then I will repent of the good wherewith I said I will benefit them.*

Here there is a light, by which one may read the history of the world with great clearness and advantage, a key to the interpretation of many volumes of the divine providence otherwise inscrutable. There is clearly the reason of the instability of human things, and the secret of those perpetual overturnings amidst kingdoms and empires, the record of which forms the great body of the annals of all history. Human affairs are unstable because they do not please God, they are not in accordance with his will, and they must be changed until they become so. When they become so, then there shall be rest and permanence among the nations; but at present there is no peace, nor any possibility of it.

The proposition that God is governor among the nations, it would seem as if no man in his senses could possibly deny. A man might as well disbelieve that God made the world, as that God governs it. And yet the doctrine of a divine superintending providence, the doctrine of God's personal presence and agency in the affairs of this world, although it be so clearly revealed in the Scriptures, has the smallest possible hold upon men's minds. Even among Christians there is but a very indefinite knowledge or belief of its truth. And among men of the world, among the nations at large, there is such a practical disregard and denial of it, and of the divine proprietary claim in human affairs, that the honest assertion and application of it in any deliberative public assembly is very likely to be ridiculed as the dotage of a superstitious mind.

There is a perpetual practical atheism among men, so that however God may be acknowledged as the object of individual worship, he is, in fact, thrust out, in men's minds, from the world of his creation. And in truth the nations are so accustomed to regard existence as merely earthly in its principles, purposes, and enjoyments, and to attach a sense of truth, value and importance only to things connected with their temporal interests, that there has come to be a complete divorce between the maxims of worldly expediency and those of Christianity, a relinquishment of temporal and state policy to the god of this world. That very expression, the god of this world, shows most impressively the world's condition in rebellion against its Maker. The spirit of rebellion runs through the whole body of its international law and policy, and infects even the volumes of its domestic statutes. This is so very generally the case, that the individual conscience is warped by it, and men come to inquire in reference to a particular employment, decision, or line of conduct, not,—Is it right? Is it in accordance with God's will?—but, Is it legal? Human law, law suggested and promulgated by the god of this world, is often thus enthroned in the place of God to the conscience.

The laws for the protection and maintenance of the system of slavery are a striking example of this fact. The law of divorce is another. Nothing can be more explicit than the legislation of our blessed Lord on this subject. *"Whosoever shall put away his wife, saving for the cause of fornication, causeth her to commit adultery; and whosoever shall marry her that is put away, committeth adultery."* And in the apparently extreme strictness of this provision, it cannot be doubted that the Divine Being pursued the very course which he knew to be requisite, if he would regulate and train society to its most perfect state of order and happiness. Now the statutes in nearly all our courts are utterly neglectful of this revealed law, if not point-blank contrary to it. In some of them a divorce can be obtained for so slight a reason, that if you were to draw your conclusions of the sacredness of the marriage contract from such legislation, the harem usages of the Turks would be quite as respectable.

This supreme enthronement of human law is sanctioned sometimes, even by the professed and public expositors of the divine law, declaring, in particular cases of iniquitous legislation, cases where the human and divine governments clash, that we ought to obey men rather than God, inasmuch as the powers that be are ordained of God, and therefore in obeying men we do obey God! With what vast displeasure must the Divine Being look upon such a condition of things, existing in the world even under the light of revelation! There was a period when nothing better could be expected, and the times of this ignorance God winked at, but now commandeth all men everywhere to repent.

No nation, in its national capacity, has yet been brought under the full influence of the divine law. Perhaps the Sandwich Islands come nearer to such a realization of Christianity than any other community; but the Baptism of the Nations has never yet taken place. A glorious spectacle indeed it would be, if any one kingdom, even the smallest, basest, most despised, should become so imbued with divine grace, so subjected by the principles of allegiance and love to God, as to regard him in all its operations; to serve him as a reflex picture on earth of angelic obedience in the hierarchies of heaven; devoting its revenues to the accomplishment of his purposes; sending out its ships for missionary enterprise and discovery, and regulating its policy with other nations by a celestial disinterestedness and nobleness of principle.

What a blessed picture for the imagination of a sanctified mind to dwell upon, could we think of this country, for example, with a government like the constitution of a holy family for its simplicity and sacredness, its governmental altar of prayer and praise morning and evening, a sentiment of sincere love to God in all hearts connected with it, and a sacred regard to the divine glory in all the circumstances of its policy. This indeed is supposing the consummation of blessedness to the world. It would be the Savior's prayer illustrated and fulfilled, *"Thy kingdom come, thy will be done on earth as it is in heaven."* It would be the realization of the brightest visions of prophecy. It would be God governing among the nations. And this would be that union of Church and State which will spring inevitably from the presence of the Spirit of the Lord. Not the embrace, legislation and protection of the Church by the State, but the adoption and sanctification of the State as a portion of the Church— the unity, and not the mere union of both. To this, it is to be hoped, all things are tending; we know that they are in the end, when the times of the restitution of all things spoken by the prophets shall have come ; and we have fondly hoped that this blissful era was near, even at the doors. But if we were to stop where we are now, little or no advance has been made towards that millennium of glory, in which the kingdoms of this world shall have become the kingdoms of our Lord, and of his Christ. What, at present, is the State? An engine of worldly, selfish, atheistic, and often reckless, oppressive and despotic policy and expediency. What ought it to be? An institution as sacredly regardful of God's glory, and of man's highest happiness, as the Church itself.

Chapter 2
Principles Of Goo's Dealings With The Nations

There can be no doubt that God deals with nations on the same principles as with individuals. The application of his laws is the same. Their accountability to him is the same. The principles of truth, holiness and justice, in each direction, are the same. Morality is not one thing in an individual, and a different thing in a nation. A nation may, by its own statutes, render a course of conduct lawful, but it cannot make it right. There may be legality, even in hell, under the laws of Satan's dominion; but not righteousness.

Then, too, the dispensations of God's providence are as definitely, and with as much selection and meaning, directed toward the nations as to individuals. They too are under a system of discipline mingled out of the treasures of mercy and chastisement. They have a life to lead, a career to run, a probation to accomplish. The means of usefulness, the opportunities of happiness, are placed at their disposal. They have a collective moral agency and obligation, a national as well as an individual conscience, and a national obedience to it, or violation of it. The national existence and responsibility is not a mere figment of the mind, not a mere collection of individual responsibilities and existences, but a great and awful reality, and as such God deals with it. As such he has provided for it a system of principles and statutes in his Word, a revelation to the nations as well as to individuals.

I am glad to justify this position by the declaration of a very profound and original thinker, though neither theologian nor statesman, (the author of the Aids to Reflection) that, *"as the New Testament sets forth the means and conditions of spiritual convalescence, with all the laws of conscience relative to our future state and permanent being, so does the Bible present to us the elements of public prudence, instructing us in the true causes, the surest preventives, and the only cure, of public evils. The authorities of Raleigh, Clarendon and Milton, must at least exempt me from the blame of singularity, if, undeterred by the contradictory charges of paradoxy from one party, and of adherence to vulgar and old-fashioned prejudices from the other, I persist in avowing my conviction that the inspired poets, historians, and sententiaries of the Jews are the clearest teachers of political economy: in short, that their writings are the Statesman's Best Manual, not only as containing the first principles and ultimate grounds of State policy, whether in prosperous times, or in those of danger and distress, but as supplying likewise the details of their application, and as being a full and spacious repository of precedents and facts in proof."*

It follows, of course, that the responsibilities and duties of nations, as of individuals, are commensurate with their capabilities, opportunities, and mercies. These all are the result of God's sovereign disposing Providence. *"He hath made of one blood all the nations of men, for to dwell on all the face of the earth, and hath determined the times before appointed, and the bounds of their habitation, that they should seek the Lord."*

All circumstances wherein they differ, all forms of language, all convergences of events, all inventions and discoveries, all varieties of climate, all aspects of earth and heaven, all things and influences that may train them up to glory and happiness, he dispenses to each as he pleases, just as he allots the gifts and varies the circumstances of individual life. To one nation he gives one talent, to another two, to another five or ten, so that nations as well as individuals are but the stewards of his mercies, for the use of which he will require a strict account.

It was a saying of Mr. Coleridge that the word privilege is the correlative of the word duty; in other language, that every privilege has a corresponding duty connected with it. This is true; for if no other duty were required but that of gratitude, every privilege from the greatest to the least, involves that, and indeed gratitude to God comprehends every duty. All our mercies are foundations of responsibility, and the greater they are, the greater our obligations become, and the more God expects of us. This is in every respect as true of nations as of individuals. It is as solemn and awful a thing, whether for a man or for a nation, to be greatly favored of God, as it is to be greatly tried and afflicted. The enjoyments of civil and religious liberty, of the opportunities of education, of the word of God, of the Christian Sabbath and the Gospel in its purity, lay a mighty weight of obligation upon any people; they trace a pathway of responsibility and duty, in which a failure must be as dreadful as success is glorious.

These principles are exhibited and sanctioned, not only in the whole course of the Divine discipline with the Jews, that people whom God seemed to have selected as a lasting example of the operation of his laws in their application to the nations, but in definite and very frequent passages of Scripture. The climax of national blessings enjoyed among the Jews, was the possession of the written word of God. "He showeth his word unto Jacob, his statutes and his judgments unto Israel. He hath not dealt so with any nation." But then, in consequence of this discipline of mercy, came another discipline, introduced by their abuse of it. *"You only have I known of all the nations of the earth; Therefore You Will I Punish For All Your Iniquities."* And precisely the same strictness of judgment is applied by our blessed Lord to communities in his own day, which, in their disobedience and rejection of the Gospel had manifested a greater degree of wickedness, than the most ancient and depraved among the cities of the Gentiles. *"Woe unto thee Chorarzin! woe unto thee Bethsaida! And thou, Capernaum, which art exalted unto heaven, shalt be brought down to hell: for if the mighty works which have been done in thee had been done in Sodom, it would have remained until this day."*

And if the pages of revelation had been continued down to modern times, and the names of other nations had been recorded visibly in the places which, though unrecorded and invisible to us, they do actually occupy in the scale of God's discipline of judgment, we should have had a history of the world as full of sacred instruction in the retributive interpositions of God, marked out and noticed for us> as ever was the history of the Hebrews in the highest and most instructive inspiration of its pages. Touched by such enchantment, the profane and atheistic atmosphere of a work like Gibbon's would have been filled with angels to our view, the revealed and busy messengers and causes of divinely appointed degradation and decay.

Chapter 3
Nature And Execution Of The Divine Retributive Providences

We are brought to the consideration of our fourth proposition, that the disregard and violation of the principles we have been contemplating will be followed by the divine retribution, and if persisted in, must result in national degradation and ruin. *"The Nation And Kingdom That WILL NOT SERVE THEE SHALL PERISH; yea, those nations shall be utterly wasted."* This most absolute and tremendous declaration may be accomplished in two ways. First, there is a connection as natural and inevitable between the evil courses of nations and their own destruction, as between the iniquities and the miseries of individuals. If, therefore, God shall speak concerning any nation as concerning his people of old: *"Israel would none of me, so I gave them up unto their own hearts' lusts, and they walked in their own counsels*:"—then the destiny of that nation is settled, its race is run.

For doubtless there is no more possibility of the repentance of a nation, except the divine grace intervene, than there is of an individual. And therefore no farther penal infliction, or retributive justice, is really requisite on the part of the Divine Being, than just to leave a nation in the unrestrained indulgence of its sins. Luxury, avarice, pride, injustice, cruelty, work the overthrow of empires, as well as the fiat of the Almighty. They are sometimes the very means of fulfilling that fiat, the very accomplishment of God's predictions of evil against a disobedient people. These dreadful ministers of wrath work with so much certainty, except repentance for the iniquity that issued their commission intervene, that oftentimes you may read its fate in the countenance of a nation, as palpably as you may the death of the drunkard in his fiery features. It needs no divine inspiration in such a case to paint the judgment of an evil kingdom; the sins of the people are the prophets of their coming woes.

On the other hand, if governments are luxurious and selfish, then there is a case pending not only between them and God, but between them and the people; in the progress of things, the people must inevitably be victorious, and those forms of empire have insured their destruction. So far as the constitution and the measures of human governments run counter to God's word, they also run counter to the interests of mankind; they oppose a perfect state of society; they maintain causes of discontent and revolution.

There is this selfish disregard to the ordinances of God and the interests of the subject all over the world. There is at the same time a ceaseless struggle towards happiness and rest, an instinctive, irrepressible tendency and movement in the chaos of society towards order, in the prison of society towards liberty; but the divine order being the only possible one, the existence of this is impossible, so long as the maxims of worldly governments move contrary to the principles of God's word; and the divine liberty being the only possible one, the enjoyment of this is impossible, so long as the people themselves are undisciplined and vile. In the eloquent language of Edmund Burke, "*It is written in the eternal constitution of things that men of intemperate minds cannot be free. THEIR PASSIONS FORGE THEIR FETTERS.*"

Until, therefore, the word of God becomes both the rule of the citizen and the Statesman's Manual, the volcanoes of political revolution will continue to disgorge their fires. The prediction runs with the reality, and is the assertion of a necessary principle. "*I will overturn, overturn, overturn, till He shall come, whose right it is, and I will give it Him.*"

There is also, in the second place, a direct, divine retribution. It has been remarked that this world is the judgment place for national sins. There is truth in this; and yet it is in the power of God in the future world to mete out strict and impartial justice to nations as well as individuals, and to make the universe see and admire the process. God knows the precise share of every individual in forming the character and conduct of the nations, and whatever the amount of guilt contracted by any nation at any given period, or through its whole existence, he can assign to each individual of all the millions of its inhabitants his exact proportion, and whatever be the punishment due, he can distribute its sufferance in the same manner. This is the only way conceivable in which the judgment of nations in eternity could be conducted. The judgment of individuals themselves must be in some sense a national judgment, since it is by individuals that every national crime is deliberated upon, and carried into execution. The making of unjust laws and treaties is an act of national guilt, in which it is very easy to see how every individual concerned in passing and executing such enactments may be arraigned and punished in eternity. The appropriation to individuals of the guilt incurred in maintaining those laws is a more difficult thing. As in individuals, so in nations, acts and habits of sin, with their consequences, are more easily avoided before they are committed, or inwrought into the system, than repented of and renounced afterwards. It is easy for one man to kindle a conflagration, which a thousand cannot master.

The life of a nation is a unity and continuity of generations. It is made up of a stream of existence, in which you cannot mark the point where one generation begins and another ends; like a woven fabric, in which you cannot tell where one thread ends or passes into another. There are habits of feeling, opinion and conduct, therefore, that belong to the same nation for ages, and in reference to which the whole continuous stream of generations from beginning to end must be judged, just as the responsibility of every part of a man's course of conduct is his own through his whole life. Then again the sins which a nation completes in one generation may have been resolved upon and commenced in another; it would therefore be manifestly unjust to judge merely that part of the existence of the nation into which the actual commission of the crime fell, while the previous generation is left unjudged or unpunished. If, for example, our own nation were now to be judged for the sin of slavery, and punished to the uttermost, we cannot suppose that this would be all, or that the share of the previous generation in permitting and entailing this guilt would be unnoticed.

In this world the retributive consequences of national guilt are not experienced sometimes till all the actors have passed from the stage of existence. While they lived, the nation might have been enjoying the fruits of its fraud, tyranny, injustice, as yet uninterrupted by the retributive providence of God, so that when that providence at length is unfolded, not a being may remain in existence, who bore any part, direct or indirect, in the commission of those crimes. This is mysterious, but not more so than the visiting the iniquities of the fathers upon the children. In such cases it is not to be supposed that the generation of actual sinners, who died while flourishing like a green bay tree, have escaped the divine vengeance. That part of the nation certainly must be judged in eternity, and one ground of judgment will be the miseries they have entailed upon posterity. Now it is no more inconsistent with the justice of the divine government that posterity should suffer for the sins of a nation, than that children should suffer for the sins of their parents, or an innocent wife and family for the drunkenness of the husband. In all such cases it is to be remembered that the suffering inflicted, though produced by the sins of others, falls, not upon the guiltless, but upon those who deserve it all and more than all, on account of their own sins, and oftentimes by similar transgressions.

Something of this is to be regarded in the denunciation of our Savior against Jerusalem. *"That upon you may come all the righteous blood shed upon the earth from the blood of righteous Abel to the blood of Zacharias. Verily I say unto you, it shall be required of this generation."* This was not saying that preceding generations would escape, but simply that the crisis, in which the divine retributions were to be experienced in this world, was deferred till the measure of iniquity should be full; and those crimes for which, from generation to generation vengeance had been denounced, but no repentance exercised, were at length all visited upon an unrepenting generation, who themselves were guilty of the greatest crime in the whole annals of the race.

'The retributive providence of God is sometimes evolved in the sure though distant operations of natural causes, which he does not interpose to prevent; as, for example, the unjust conquests of the Romans were followed by the introduction of habits that led to the ruin of the empire. And the iniquitous conduct of Spain, in the discovery and possession of the South American continent, though for a time it filled the nation with wealth, is, by natural causes, connected with her present miseries. Just so, an unjust accumulation of wealth by individuals, though it may go unpunished during a man's lifetime, is not unfrequently followed by evil courses in his children; the sins of the fathers are visited upon the children, in being made the progenitors of their sins; with their own concurrence, certainly, and a guilty concurrence, but not the less a visitation, and a dreadful one, from

God; for had those parents been virtuous, then those very same children, in all likelihood, had been virtuous also. And this proverb, "*he that is greedy of gain troubleth his own house*," is as true of nations, as it is of individuals.

The retributive providence of God may be prevented by repentance, nor would it, in any of those cases where it has been so signally and awfully illustrated, have received such an illustration, if repentance had intervened. "*At what instant I shall speak concerning a nation, and concerning a kingdom, to pluck up and pull down, and destroy it, if that nation against whom I have pronounced, turn from their evil, I WILL REPENT OF THE EVIL THAT I THOUGHT TO DO UNTO THEM.*" Here stands out a great and most merciful provision in God's national statute book. Sincere repentance prevents the threatened evil, in nations as well as individuals. There is, besides, another wondrous shield that stands between God's wrath and the nation that deserves it, and that is his own constituted church, and the prayers of his redeemed people. The Sodoms and Gomorrahs of our day would doubtless flame up to heaven in their ruin, as they cry up to heaven in their sins, were it not for the righteous men, that by God's grace, instead of five or ten, answer his requisition to Abraham sometimes by hundreds and thousands. How beautifully is this truth conveyed in those lines of the poet Cowper, which I love to repeat and dwell upon, descriptive of the world's dependence, for its happy existence, upon the living presence of the Christian!—

> "Perhaps the self-approving haughty world,
> That, as she sweeps him with her whistling silks,
> Scarce deigns to notice him, or, if she see,
> Deems him a cypher in the works of God,
> Receives advantage from his noiseless hours,
> 'Of which she little dreams. Perhaps she owes
> Her sunshine and her rain, her blooming spring,
> And plenteous harvest, to the prayer he makes,
> When, Isaac-like, the solitary saint
> Walks forth to meditate at eventide,
> And think on her, who thinks not for herself."

Sometimes the Church herself becomes participator in the sins of a rebellious people, and then the shield against God's wrath proves its conductor. It is a fearful climax of evil when this is the case. This, in truth, especially in the Oriental world, reads the history of more than one nation, once Christian, but now blotted from existence, or lost in heathenism.

Sometimes the long suffering of God is carried so far, that it seems as if there were no cognizance taken of national crimes, iniquities being committed at which the heavens and the earth cry out for their enormity, and yet God's justice sleeps. This makes the nations hardy in their sins; they laugh at the predictions of God's wrath, and scornfully ask, where is the promise of his coming? The Antediluvians did this, and when Enoch preached with such prodigious eloquence and power, like the outpouring of the seven vials, his predictions of the deluge of divine vengeance, he was assailed with the fury of unbelief and wrath. The facility with which nations become atheists in their public capacity, and scorn the idea that God interposes in human affairs, is partly because some mighty and astounding interposition, enough to compel the awe of the universe, does not take place in their own generation. They are more obtuse in their discernment, and blind in their unbelief than hardened individuals, and the most terrific of the divine judgments being sometimes slow in their progress, and unperceived, unnoticed, except by spiritual observers, have little power to arrest the deep tide of profligacy. They are the more dreadful because unrecognized.

God's retributive providence may be invisible as the angel of death, and gradual as the remorseless tide that steals its march for centuries, or the malaria that depopulates cities, and makes the very sight of them the dread of the traveler. One might, with almost as much impunity, go into the tomb of a plague-stricken mortal, as linger among the beautiful remains of some of those buried cities, whose inquest would rightly be written, Died By The Visitation Of God!—and yet that visitation unknown and unacknowledged even by the sufferers. Sometimes a series of retributive providences is unfolded, no one of which, by itself, excites alarm or surprise, till in the lapse of ages the solemn work is done, the nation has passed from existence, and historians write its epitaph, and philosophize upon the causes of its fall. A lingering decay may be far worse than a sudden overthrow; so that, in such a case, the common lamentation of mankind may be deeper for the degradation that remains, than the glory that has departed. It is the same with individuals. And this perhaps was the meaning of that melancholy breathing of the poet:—

> "Thus fares it still in our decay;
> And yet the wiser mind
> Mourns less for what age takes away,
> Than what it leaves behind."

A nation dies when the spirit of everything good and noble dies in it. The name may live, when the elements of life and beauty have departed. God may suffer the sins which a nation is cherishing to consume its energies, till the gangrene becomes incurable, and then his abused mercies work their own revenge. How solemn, in such a case, are the records and the proofs of the divine indignation—the prediction and the fulfillment seen and read together!

I have stood beneath the walls of the Coliseum in Rome, the Parthenon in Athens, and the Temple of Karnak in Egypt:— each of them the mighty relic of majestic empires, and the symbol of the spirit of the most remarkable ages in the world. The last, carrying you back as in a dream over the waste of four thousand years, might be supposed to owe its superior impressiveness to its vast antiquity; but that is not the secret of the strange and solemn thoughts that crowd into the mind; it is the demonstration of God's wrath fulfilled according to the letter of the Scriptures! No ruins of antiquity are so overwhelming in their interest as the gigantic remains of that empire, once the proudest in the world, and now, according to the very letter of the divine prediction, *"the basest of the kingdoms."* From the deep and grim repose of those sphinxes, obelisks, and columns,—those idols broken at the presence of God,—as the mind wanders back to the four hundred years of Israel's bondage in Egypt, methinks you may hear the wail of that old and awful prophecy, with the lingering echo of every successive prediction— THE NATION WHOM THEY SHALL SERVE WILL I JUDGE! Who would have believed it possible, four thousand years ago, amidst the vigor and greatness of the Egyptian kingdom, that after that vast lapse of time, travelers should come from a world then as new, unpeopled, and undiscovered, as the precincts of another planet, to read the proofs of God's veracity in the vestiges at once of such stupendous glory and such a stupendous overthrow! And now, if any man, contemplating the youthful vigor, the energy, the almost indestructible life of our own country, finds it difficult to believe that the indulgence of the same national sin, under infinitely clearer light, may be followed with a similar overthrow, let him wander on the banks of the Nile, and think down hours to moments in the silent sanctuaries of its broken temples.

Chapter 4
Elements Of National Gratitude And Responsibility, The Word Of God, The Christian Sabbath, A Converted Ministry, The Holy Spirit, A Good Government, Freedom Of Opinion, Common Schools

We are now prepared to realize the truth of our fifth proposition, that the enumeration and acknowledgment of the causes of national gratitude is an exceedingly solemn service. It becomes so just in proportion to the number and importance of our blessings. What then are the elements of national gratitude? We can notice but a few of the most important, but in doing this we shall find a most impressive picture of our own national responsibilities. The first to be mentioned is the possession of the word of God, in our own language, and without restriction on the reading or the publication of it. Let any man travel in Catholic countries, and he will feel the importance of the two latter adjuncts of this blessing. To possess the Scriptures, but in a dead and foreign tongue, is, for the mass of the people, equivalent to being deprived of them. To possess them in the vernacular, but with the ban of the church against their perusal, is, if possible, still worse. The free gift of the Holy Scriptures to any people is one, the greatness of which, as of the responsibilities connected with it, is not to be described in language.

Next to this blessing is that of the Christian Sabbath; and connected with it, the gospel preached in its purity by a holy and enlightened ministry. The word of God itself would do us little good, if the Sabbath were blotted from existence, or if the constituted expounders and teachers of the word were unconverted men, or falsifiers of its doctrines. Without doubt the gospel is preached in this country with a simplicity and plainness more accordant with its nature, and by men more generally of experimental piety, than in any other country in the world. The greatness of this blessing, again, we cannot adequately appreciate. The gift of the Holy Spirit, in connection with the proclamation of the gospel, is another vast and incalculable blessing, without which indeed, those already mentioned, though they might benefit the temporal condition of our race, would be of no avail for their highest interests. The effusion of the Spirit of God, to render divine truth effectual in the conversion of men, is the culminating gift in the series of blessings purchased by the crucifixion of the Savior. It is the last object of prayer, the only possible ground of the advancement of the Redeemer's Kingdom, the only hope of individual or national salvation.

In the continued outpouring of the Spirit, and the revivals of religion consequent upon it, we are enjoying the highest possible proof of the divine favor, the highest possible assurance of our country's safety, and the highest possible means of usefulness. Our moral power over the nations is increased and enhanced in an incalculable degree, and our preparation for the mighty part which we fondly hope God destines our nation to take in the world's evangelization, must become, by the continuance of this blessing, well-nigh perfect. Our responsibilities are greater than those of any other nation, just in proportion as we precede the rest of the world in the enjoyment of this new and marvelous element of national gratitude, the Baptism of the Spirit.

These are the four highest elements of mercy and responsibility, our four greatest blessings, because they are religious blessings, and constitute, in their union, the perfect gift of our religion. Three other elements may be named, comprehending our political and social interests.

A wise and good government well administered. A government may be good in its constitution, but spoiled in its administration. It may be evil in its constitution, and therefore evil in its administration, even though conducted with all the wisdom and benevolence of which it is capable; and it may be both bad in itself and badly administered. Most governments in the world come under this last description, for they have generally been but so many organized systems of despotism and oppression; the power and luxury of the few, built upon the crushed minds, hearts, and hopes of the many. In such a world of violence and misrule, a good government is a gift of

God's mercy of inappreciable value, an element of national gratitude and responsibility as precious as it is rare. A good government is an essential requisite for a grand and lasting instrumentality in the world's evangelization. Most governments are so wicked in their very essence, that the kingdom of Christ will have to be established on their ruins. Now we think it must be admitted that there are fewer evils in the theory and administration of the government of this [country than of any other in the world. It is perhaps the best adapted to the growth of a people in knowledge, usefulness, and holiness. At any rate, in comparison with the unhappy constitution of other governments, it is of such supreme excellence and blessedness, as to constitute for us an immense ground of thanksgiving and responsibility.

A sixth element of national gratitude is freedom of opinion. I mention this as being the surest index and the most important result of civil and religious liberty. We can scarcely appreciate this blessing in our own country, for, like the air that we breathe, it has been round about us from our infancy. But the pages of history are a perpetual record of wars and persecutions on account of opinion. Political opinions, religious opinions, and even philosophical opinions, when they have been supposed to run counter to the tenets of the Church, have been prosecuted as crimes. Our discourse would be filled with names only, should we attempt to enumerate even a small part in the list of the martyrs of opinion. But are not all men free to think? it may be asked. Yes! as much as a prisoner in his cell is free to go the length of his chain, or to walk from one wall to the other. But can outward shackles or threats of persecution stop the freedom of opinion? Most assuredly. They induce the habit of slavish thinking; they make the mind's habitual state a state of bondage; they make it think, not freely, but according to received rules and dogmas, and paths traced out. The interdict against the free publication of opinion is an interdict also upon the formation of opinion, for it is as true, as it is beautifully expressed, that –

> Thoughts shut up want air,
> And spoil, like bales unopened to the sun:

-- and so, in a very short time there will be no wholesome thought at all. The mind suffocates in such a prison, just as a light, put beneath an air-tight receiver, is extinguished. Even in this country, free as it is, there is yet the element of bondage and of persecution. Even here there are so many adverse influences, that in making your investigations in dark quarters with the torch of truth, you need to have a safety lamp, like Sir Humphrey Davy's invention, which you may thrust, with its light, into the midst of the impurest gases, or the moment it touches them they will blow you up. Still, there is a freedom of opinion in this country greater and more absolute than any where in the world. It constitutes a most important element in our causes of national thanksgiving.

The seventh and last element, which I shall mention, is that of good common schools. I take this as the criterion of excellence and universality in a national education. No language can tell the greatness of this blessing. In the possession and the right use of it, any country would rise to greatness and prosperity. Good common schools, the common schools of New-England, are a mighty and blessed discipline to the mind, the heart, the conscience. They put the elements of power into every hand, and teach every mind to govern them. It were to be wished that a vast deal more of care and attention were devoted to them in this state and city. We have only to step over into England, and we may there see, for want of that common blessing of our land, common schools, the benefit of that other great blessing, Sabbath schools, in a great degree unknown. For the Sabbath school in England is merely two hours of the common day school of this country turned into the Sabbath, to give to the poor the miserable apology for that inestimable blessing, from the enjoyment of which they are excluded during the week.* Note A.

Note A
It has been a melancholy consequence of the neglect of common school education in England, that the sacredness of the Sabbath should have to be violated in teaching the most common rudiments of knowledge. "*Some of our friends of the independent class,*" says a member of the committee in an attempted vindication of this system in one of the large cities, "*have forsaken us because we teach writing and accounts on Sundays. We would willingly teach these on week-day evenings, but the factory hands work so late that we have found. it impracticable; therefore we put this on the score of works of ne-*

cessity and mercy, considering our Savior as sanctioning the pulling out of sheep from the pit on the Sabbath."

The difficulty is, that they themselves put the sheep into the pit on the week-days, and on the same days should do the work of pulling them out. Here is the spectacle of the richest nation in the world tasking its immortal energies so fearfully in the pursuit of wealth, as not to allow its children time to gain the lowest rudiments of education! Working them in the service of mammon all the week, and then stealing a portion of the season of spiritual rest to shut them up to the study of writing and arithmetic!

It is a good element in our common school instruction that it is not sectarian. And it ought never to become so. In countries the least enlightened, and the most despotic, it is; the genius of the Roman Catholic religion makes it so. And, truly, I wonder that the advocates of that religion in this country should have had so little of their wonted sagacity as to be willing to expose and obtrude into notice so obnoxious a feature in their system. I wonder that they do not also claim that a particular portion of heaven's atmosphere be walled up from the rest of the canopy that overhangs our city, and consecrated to their exclusive possession. The air that we breathe is not more the free, unmortgaged, unprejudiced, and equal property of all, than ought to be the element of common school instruction.* Note B

Note B
The question as to the alienation of a portion of the school fund in this state from a common and impartial to a sectarian disposal has been happily set at rest for the present, and we trust will never again even be looked at. The proposition was one, which we really believe if it had come from any other sect than that of the Catholics, would have been treated with contempt, as a most rampant and disgusting exhibition of bigotry. It has been remarked with equal severity and justice, that *"the conduct of the priests and leading men in holding Irish catholic meetings, for the purpose of subverting the institutions of this country, and getting possession of its school funds, its impudence of no ordinary cast, and shows that something has stultified their perceptions. What scorn would Americans justly bring upon the monasteries of Spain, or the domestic institutions of any other country of Europe. What scorn, if instead of sending missionaries unarmed to teach justice and temperance from the Bible, they should send their ships of war to force Protestantism and brandy on the heathen at the cannon's mouth!"* This allusion to the tyranny exercised over the Sandwich Is-

lands in the violent introduction and establishment of the Roman Catholic religion, with the trade in brandy, by the aid of French ships of war is appropriate. Who can doubt that similar measures would be pursued for the same ends by the same sect in this country, if it were but sufficiently powerful?

With these grand elements of national blessedness and thanksgiving, a world might be up in arms against us, and we could stand the shock; a world might be sunk in wretchedness, and we could bless, redeem, and save it. We are bound to see to it, that we do not neutralize the power and benefit of these blessings, and the power of our own example over the nations, by the practice of iniquity among ourselves; of iniquity, perhaps, which every civilized nation under heaven has abandoned. It is to be fondly hoped that God will not permit us so to thwart his goodness. In the atrocious iniquity committed by the English nation in its attack upon the Chinese Empire, for the defense of the privilege of poisoning the natives of that Empire with smuggled opium, we can see how far even a professedly Christian people may go in acts that renders its moral power over others a nullity and a laughing stock.

We are bound to avoid such monstrous inconsistencies, and not only to take care, for ourselves, of the blessings God has bestowed upon us, but to use them as the means of blessedness to the world. We are bound to watch over, for ourselves and others, the element of freedom of opinion, that it do not degenerate into licentiousness and atheism; of a free government, that it be justly administered; of common schools, that they be well taught and everywhere provided for; of the word of God, that it be everywhere disseminated; of the Gospel, that it be preached in purity; of the Sabbath, that it be not desecrated and abused; of revivals of religion, that they be not, through the sins of the people, and the lukewarmness of the Church, permitted to cease from existence.

Perhaps there is not another nation in the world that possesses together all these elements of blessedness, these merciful tokens of God's peculiar favor. I am sure there is no other people possessing them to the degree that we do. Nor is it in the power of language to describe, or of the mind to measure, the extent of obligation and responsibility with which they load us as a nation. They open before us, and urge upon us, a career of benevolence and glory, such as no other people ever entered on, such as no other can command. They mark as distinctly a great design of God in regard to us, as if some aged prophet of the Lord—some majestic, heaven-inspired Isaiah—three thousand years ago, had written down, as in the case of Cyrus, our very name and character in the scroll of his predictions.

The thought of the possibility of a waste and abuse of these mercies, a failure of these high purposes of God in regard to us, is painful in the extreme. How much more so, if the view of our obstinately cherished sins, our forming habits, and the festering evils in our system, render it in the least degree probable. Surely, there is a voice to us, as there was to ancient Israel, from the bright array of our spiritual mercies especially, and in reference to their peculiarity— *"YOU only have I known of all the nations of the earth, therefore YOU will I punish for all your iniquities!"* And God has preserved that degraded and all but annihilated people, with the marks of his wrath upon them, in the sight of the nations, as it were like a lost archangel with the deep thunder scars of his fall entrenched in his once bright countenance, to teach surviving empires, on a most mighty and terrific scale of vengeance, the awful consequences of despised mercies, guilt persisted in, and vast responsibilities abused. Let me repeat the lesson, copied by the instructive genius of Cowper, from the pages of inspiration:

> Their glory faded, and their race dispersed,
> The last of nations now, though once the first,
> They warn and teach the proudest, would they learn,
> Keep wisdom, or meet vengeance in your turn;
> If we escaped not, if Heaven spared not us,
> Peeled, scattered, and exterminated thus;
> If vice received her retribution due,
> When we were visited, what hope for you 1
> When God arises, with an awful frown,
> To punish lust, or pluck presumption down,
> When gifts perverted, or not duly prized,
> Pleasure o'er valued and his grace despised,
> Provoke the vengeance of his righteous hand,
> To pour down wrath upon a thankless land,
> He will be found impartially severe,
> Too just to wink or speak the guilty clear.

"*Behold, therefore,*" says the apostle Paul, in reference to the same grand and tragic lesson;" *behold, therefore, the goodness and severity of God; on them which fell severity, but towards thee goodness, if thou continue in his goodness: Other Wise, THOU ALSO SHALT BE CUT OFF.*"

Part 2
Indications Of The Divine Providence Concerning The Destiny And Duty Of The United States

> The time of rest, the promised Sabbath, comes!
> Six thousand years of sorrow have well nigh
> Fulfilled their tardy and disastrous course
> Over a sinful world; and what remains
> Of this tempestuous state of human things,
> Is merely as the working of the sea
> Before a calm, that rocks itself to rest:—
> For he, whose car the winds are, and the clouds
> The dust that waits upon his sultry march,
> When sin hath moved him, and his wrath is hot,—
> Shall visit earth in mercy; shall descend
> Propitious in his chariot paved with love;
> And what his storms have blasted and defaced
> For man's revolt, shall with a smile repair.
> The Task. (Book VL)

Chapter 5
Particulars Op The Divine Providence, Our Origin, Our Government, Our Previous And Successive Discipline, Freedom From A Religious Establishment

It would be difficult to find a more solemn and definite announcement of the rule of God's providence towards us as a people, than is contained in the passage adduced at the close of the preceding chapter. There can be no doubt that it is addressed to nations as well as individuals; to the Gentile nation in contradistinction from the Jewish nation. We are admonished by the fall of the Jews, the rejection of the natural branches of the olive, to beware, lest on account of our sins, God reject us also, who at best, are only grafted in upon the original stock. For eighteen centuries the experience of nations has been commenting upon this text; and even that of England and America may yet have to be annexed to it, in the course of the divine indignation on account of national sins. Doubtless, there is ample time and verge enough within the scope of the vast circle of prophecy, for such an additional illustration of God's justice on a mighty scale. The Divine Being might make a short work upon the earth, and yet within its limits there might be traced the overthrow and destruction of a nation like our own, because of our ingratitude, and the selection and preparation of another people for the accomplishment of the Divine purposes of mercy to the world. Nevertheless, we hope that in regard both to our own and the whole world's evangelization, the commands laid upon us, are no greater than God will yet bestow the power, the willingness, and the grace to accomplish. In this hope, after the survey we have taken of the more general methods of God's providence among the nations, and of the more important elements of national gratitude and responsibility, let us now endeavor to trace a little more closely the tenor of God's discipline in regard to ourselves, and the grand divine purpose indicated by it.

Among the circumstances that combine to put a great degree of moral power into our hands, and to invest us with great responsibilities, we may enumerate the following particulars.

1. Our origin as a people has been noble. We are made out of the sternest materials the world could furnish. Our ancestry were self-denying, heroic, energetic, pious. The older the world grows, the more will it honor the name of Puritan. That title will be a synonym for all that is illustrious in patriotism, fearless in liberty, devoted in piety. Our Puritan fathers were the best spirits of England. Born in agitated times, nursed in the iron cradle of persecution, freemen of the freest country then upon earth, and freemen by a yet nobler title, with the liberty that Christ gives to his people.

A truly virtuous parentage, is the noblest inheritance of individuals. The son of Edmund Burke would have been molded by the spirit, and animated by the memory, and mantled around with the moral power of so illustrious a father. It is still nobler for a whole people.

None can tell the prodigious moral power we derive from habits induced, and sentiments instilled into the common mind in the childhood of our existence, by men that walked with God. They kept the Sabbath; and to this circumstance is owing the superior sacredness of that day's observance in this country, compared with its almost universal desecration in other countries. You may call it a prejudice, if you will, that extreme veneration of feeling and strictness of practice, but to be girded in our infancy by such prejudices, is to have an iron constitution for God's service in our manhood.

In every respect our origin imposes upon us vast obligations. It was so extraordinary as to fix upon us the gaze of nations. Born of such parents, it is demanded, it is expected, that our whole existence shall be a lofty course of freedom and piety, expansive as the world, and lasting as the continent we inhabit. Our ancestors were men of prayer. Their supplications gird us about, even now, like a wall of adamant. They offered them in faith and fervor, amidst trial and distress ; they probably behold an answer every day, in the blessings that we receive. By the power of such prayers they are, as it were, still in the midst of us, a band of righteous men, for whose sake we may be spared and redeemed, though our own guilt threatens destruction.

2. To such a discipline in our parentage God has superadded the great and blessed gift of a free government, simple in its constitution, and emanating from the people. It was necessary to prepare a people for such a gift by such a discipline. It could not have been bestowed upon any other people already in existence, and educated under the power of principles, habits, and manners, at variance with it and inadequate to its support. It grows out of and is adapted to our circumstances; our political freedom springs from our religious freedom; and a form of government beneath which any other people would run wild, or else would soon convert it into some iron form of despotism, fits us in its spirit and texture as a coat of flexible mail fits the body, and forms an instrument of prodigious power in all our movements.

We have a government that leaves us at leisure to prosecute our purposes; it is a part of ourselves. In most cases the government and the people, in theory if not in practice, are at variance, just as if the one were in essential enmity and jealousy against the other. Hostility of course arises, and nations have too much to do with their own political struggles to look after the world's spiritual interests. With us it is not so. Our government is the people's government, and in it they are secure. Whatever dispute there may be as to the theoretical merits of different forms of government, whether the monarchical or the republican form be the best, the question for us is settled by a degree of happiness and prosperity resulting from our republican constitution unexampled in the whole world.

I believe that a republic, with that preparation for it which God has granted us, is better fitted than any other form of government for the accomplishment of his spiritual purposes of mercy to the world. Its unostentatious frame-work and the simplicity of its aim, admit of a perfect alliance with the spirit and precepts of our religion. Most governments, being in their very constitution nothing but contrivances of individual or oligarchical luxury, power, and pride, the religion of the gospel cannot mingle with them, but is compelled to stand aloof, and at the uttermost can only do something to neutralize and mitigate their evil. The Baptism of the Nations will doubtless be vouchsafed to those first that are best prepared for it; and in our view a republic rightly administered constitutes a State, in which there are the fewest obstacles in the way of such a regeneration. Inveterate national prejudices, antique cherished abuses, and unjust practices indulged, constitute aground of resistance to the Holy Ghost in nations as well as individuals. The various establishments of Great Britain are opposed to such a National Baptism by the Divine Spirit as has been referred to. The simplicity of our institutions, on the other hand, favors it.

3. The discipline by which we were prepared for such a government has been followed by a discipline in its establishment equally adapted to honor and sustain it. The character of our revolution was worthy of the character and struggles of our Puritan ancestors. The same lofty principles were involved in it, and developed, and established by it, in the sight of all the world. It was a great thing, besides the blessing of a Puritan ancestry, to be honored with the gift of such a being as Washington for the second father of his country. We came into existence as an independent people under the most favorable circumstances. Our birth was not premature, nor were we rocked and dandled into manhood. We were disciplined by adversity, and had enough of storm to indurate, without breaking our frame. Our

revolutionary contest is known to have been sustained by prayer; the formation of our constitution is associated with pious recollections; for that, too, was built up under the influence of prayer. The more our history becomes known, the more we shall be expected to exhibit, wherever we go, a model of piety to God, as well as freedom and fearlessness towards man.

Our atmosphere is the natural mountain air of liberty and piety, and as fast as other nations become sufficiently enlightened and religious, our institutions, in essence and in spirit, will probably prevail. As fast as wise revolutions take place in other countries, as fast as thrones crumble, and tyranny breaks up, and the people grasp the power, they will look to us with more earnestness, and a deeper veneration. We shall have a hold on the esteem and affections of the world, which nothing but our own betrayal of their confidence by a career of crime can diminish. Our very existence, in freedom and happiness, under a government more purely popular and republican than has ever prevailed among civilized men from the beginning of the world, exerts, of itself, a power over the nations utterly incalculable. All Europe would be in a very different condition, if, from the influences that have made Europe what it is, you could abstract merely the example of the continued existence of this nation.

4. In granting us the blessing of a free government, God has also graciously separated his Church in this country, from abase and unnatural dependence on the State, and has granted us the blessing of a free and independent church organization. He has blessed us with a freedom from church establishments, such as the world has not seen, nor the church known, for many centuries. He has not permitted that politico-spiritual incubus to weigh us down; that source of pride, contention, worldliness, and vainglory to exist among us. The deliverance of the Church from this monstrous evil, it has cost longtime, and a world of patient labor to work out. It was no part even of the Reformation to accomplish this blessing. A refuge in the wilderness of this western world must be provided, and a band of holy men driven into it by persecution; and even now it is only a few years since the perfect separation of the Church from the State was accomplished in this country. The era was worthy of a place in the chronology of the most remarkable events in the world's history; for the perfection of religious freedom is as rare and wonderful a possession as

the perfection of civil freedom. Indeed, till within a few years its very existence has been supposed impossible, and what men have termed the voluntary principle, has been regarded with the utmost horror, as if it were the very annihilation of religion among men, the disorganization and destruction of all religious societies.

The idea that God has instituted a Church which cannot stand without the arm of the civil government to lean upon, is but part of that system which supposes the people to exist for the pleasure of their rulers, and not the rulers at the will and for the good of the people. Religion being the dearest of all human possessions, if the civil government can tyrannize over that, its despotism over all other things is unlimited and secure. The idea, therefore, that religion is not a great governmental establishment, but a popular and voluntary thing, annihilates an old and sanctified prejudice, and strikes down one of the strongest buttresses of tyranny. In truth, voluntary associations of any kind, contain within themselves the germ of civil and religious freedom. If men can do one thing without the intervention either of a bench of bishops or a bench of peers, they can another, so that voluntary associations do, sooner or later, carry in themselves the death warrant both of civil and ecclesiastical despotism. In the successful example and experiment of the Church in this country, a monstrous and tyrannical prejudice has been shaken and rooted from its foundation, which, under whatever goodly name or form, has filled society with persecution, bloodshed, and bondage, and which, if not overthrown, would have rendered the complete triumph of the Gospel, in the accomplishment of the world's evangelization, impossible.

To show, in one particular direction, the nature of establishments, as an obstacle against the spread of the Gospel,— the unalterable essence of the spirit of bigotry, domination, and exclusiveness connected with them,—it is enough to notice the following fact. A clergyman of the Church of England, being on heathen ground, proposed attending a prayer-meeting held by the missionaries of the American Board. He was threatened by another Episcopal clergyman, though not of the Church of England, but of this country, and it would seem outrunning even his brother of the establishment in the comprehensive energy and despotic consistency of High Church principles, that if he did dare attend the unhallowed conventicler [a secret or unlawful religious meeting, specially nonconformist views], he should be complained of to the established authorities of his Mother Church. Rather than make difficulty, the divinely ordained servant of the establishment, exorcised of the inconsistent spirit of liberality and lowliness, submissively repressed his yearnings after communion with his missionary praying brethren, and inasmuch as that was all that an establishment could there do to show its superiority, or to maintain the exclusive divine right and dignity of Episcopal ordination, left the unanointed missionaries to pray alone! Poor, forlorn, proscribed disciples! Had it been a little earlier in the world's history, instead of quietly pursuing your holy work, with silent pity for the arrogant assumptions of your brethren, and the exhibition of a spirit so inconsistent with the business of the world's conversion, you would have expiated your offence perhaps within the walls of a prison! In the good providence of God, it is mainly through the existence of a Church without an establishment in this country, that it has come to be possible for a society of Christians not only to pray alone and unmolested anywhere, but even to be honored and revered of men, and sanctioned and glorified in the descent of the Divine Spirit, though untitled, and unsanctioned, either by the seal of Pope or Bishop, King or Queen.

What could be supposed, as to the prospect of the world's evangelization, if the spirit of the gospel, instead of being that free, unshackled, benevolent, ethereal essence that it is, had been the narrow, proud, exclusive, dictatorial, persecuting, papistical spirit, that constitutes the essence of a prelatical [prelate], and,—in reference to the war it has waged against all sects not within its own bosom, I had almost said—piratical establishment! To convert this world unto Christ, a religion is needed, not of forms and ceremonies, and arrogant assumptions and titles, but a religion of humility, meekness, and love; a religion that can, if need be, become all things to all men, and not a religion which, even on heathen ground, would rather part with the spirit of the gospel itself, than relinquish a solitary jot of its unhallowed, haughty, bigoted pretensions. I regard the delineation of the New Jerusalem, in the Book of John's revelation, as a remarkable description of the nature of that religion which is to fill the world.

I Saw No Temple Therein: For The Lord God Almighty And The Lamb Are The Temple Of It. A most significant indication is here presented of the liberty, universality, and omnipresence, like the all-penetrating and surrounding air, of that worship of God, which is one day to fill the earth with its blessedness. There will be no mediatorial images, crosses, liturgies, or exclusive ceremonies, to come between the soul and God; or to monopolize and stereotype the expression of its piety; no self-assumptive titles, or arrogant pretensions to the sole divine sanction; no cathedrals or oratotories where God so exclusively abides, that none can rightly worship but within their sacred precincts; but a presence and a worship that gathers, not sects and churches merely, nor Presbyterian, nor Episcopal, nor prelatical establishments, but whole nations into its bosom!

Chapter 6
Particulars Of The Divine Providence Continued, A Regenerated And Educated Ministry, Revivals Of Religion, Prevalence Of The English Language

5. Next to the blessing of freedom from a religious establishment may be named, as fitting us for a great share in the world's evangelization, an enlightened and converted ministry, and a high standard of theological education. For the last great conflict with the powers of darkness, a ministry is needed possessing the spirit and conversant with the riches of God's word, a ministry girded with the armor of righteousness on the right hand and on the left, and of practiced skill in the use of it. Now there can be no doubt that theological education is advancing to a perfection in this country, the education both of knowledge amassed and practical experience gained, such as it has reached in no other; a circumstance that may encourage us to believe that we are destined for an instrumentality in the advancement of the Redeemer's Kingdom among the nations, not local or temporary, but universal and perpetual.

6. Next to this, and in close connection with it, is to be named the gift of the Holy Spirit in revivals of religion. Year after year we may hope they are becoming wider, deeper, more constant. We may hope in the divine mercy, that throughout the nation this leaven of blessedness will continue to work, till the whole is leavened; nay, we have some reason to believe that God will make even us, as a people, his first example of a great nation wholly penetrated with the influence, and obedient to the principles of Divine Grace. At any rate, the moral power which revivals of religion continued must give, is immense; the responsibility they lay upon us cannot be conceived. To what extent it may please God to work speedily, in the same glorious manner, in other countries, we cannot tell; we may hope he is preparing the way; and doubtless, if we are humble and prayerful, he will continue the blessing to us, and make revivals here the forerunners and

instruments in producing them elsewhere. Thus, while religion flourishes at home, our religious power abroad will be magnified to a gigantic extent. As the fountain deepens and widens here, we may multiply its streams throughout the earth; not only to carry salvation to the heathen, but to refresh, invigorate, and purify the old and corrupt establishments of all Christendom.

Our revivals are a display of God's mercy and grace, that already has stirred up the dormant energies of the English church, and has excited the wonder, the investigation, the prayers, and the imitation of pious men throughout Great Britain. Then, too, the greatest revival of religion in modern times, the revival in the Sandwich Islands, has taken place by God's mercy, under the instrumentality of our missionaries. The influence of these things must be felt, wherever they are heard of, and the transaction of religious phenomena so wonderful, so glorious, will make the nations be looking for a vast increase of our pious enterprise and activity. And while these effusions of the Spirit must, of necessity, rouse such an expectation, they will give us the power, provided we keep at the foot of the cross, where only our safety lies, amply to fulfill it. They are, indeed, a consolation amidst all our fears; they call for unceasing gratitude to God, of whose patience, forbearance, and infinite compassion, they are so astonishing an exhibition. Notwithstanding the dark signs of the times, they hold out to us the animating hope, that he designs this country to be yet the main instrument in the world's regeneration; and that he is beginning to prepare the American church, by a vast access to her numbers, elevation of her purity, and increase of her light, for the magnificent scale of exertion on which her enterprises are hereafter to be conducted.

7. We speak a language containing vast treasures of religious wisdom, and vernacular, more or less, over a large portion of the globe, and for this and other causes, perhaps destined to become an organ of international communication more universal than any other tongue. The students at the missionary seminary at Basle in Germany, well denominated the English language the missionary language. It might almost be called the language of religion, in reference to the vast treasures of theological science, the mines of religious truth, and above all, the inestimable works of practical piety, of which it furnishes the key. There is in it a capital of speculative and practical

theology, rich and deep enough for the whole world to draw upon. From time to time, God himself has especially honored it, and prepared it more and more for his glory, by giving to the world, through its medium, such works as the Pilgrim's Progress and the Paradise Lost. It is the language of Protestantism, the language of civil and religious freedom, the language of commercial enterprise, the language spoken by the greater portion of seamen in the world. It is the language of the two freest, most enterprising, most powerful, and so far as the appellation can at present be admitted in a national sense, most truly Christian nations on the globe.

The English tongue owes so much of its power and beauty to the Scriptures, that for this reason alone it is almost a sanctified instrument for the Church to work with. The common translation of the Bible, both in Germany and England, exerted the most beneficial influence in molding the language, as well as the mind and morals of the people. Perhaps it has done more in the formation of our language, and the preservation of its purity, than all other causes. Bunyan is the most remarkable example of its agency in the development of genius. It was his intense study of the English Bible that gave him the command of a style of such native, idiomatic, simplicity and beauty. For him the Scriptures were his mind's sole storehouse, both of words and images, and his sensibilities opened beneath their influence, as the flowers open to the sun. To the same ennobling inspiration the greatest of the English poets were indebted almost as much as he. So were the best prose-writers. Their minds were all baptized in the same cloud of glory, and all passed through the same invigorating, shining sea. And indeed, if we could suppose the whole of that part of British literature drawn away, which, in thought and imagination, in feeling and energy, sprung from the same fountain, there would remain hardly the skeleton of its living beauty. It would be like the lifeless, inexpressive canvass of a vast painting, from which you have destroyed the whole perspective, and blotted out the imaginative lights and shades.

Taking all these influences into consideration, there is not another language in the world so sacred, so connected with holy associations, and, for the treasures of religion which it embalms, so important to man's highest interests, as the English language. We therefore cannot but regard its increasing prevalence as a great and special indication of the providence of God. The time is not far distant, other causes being supposed to maintain their influence, when this language shall have become an organ for the world's literature; and in addition to this, if we mistake not, the world's religious bookmart, and most elevated and important literary center, will be found in America. The probability of this will be made more evident in the light of the next grand topic in our enumeration.

Chapter 7
Enumeration Continued, Rapid Increase Of Our Population, Our Common School Education, Our Relative Geographical Position

8. The immense population, speaking the English language, which is soon to swell the census of the United States, is another point of God's providence and discipline towards us, of incalculable importance. It gives to every other consideration a hundred fold weight in our view. It gives magnitude even to trifles. The tide of our population rolls on with tremendous rapidity and power. When Mr. Evarts committed the last gift of his devoted spirit to the church of Christ in this country, in that sublime, prophetic, and almost inspired production, on the *Moral Destiny of the United States*, he made the calculation, based on the safest and most probable positions, that in one hundred and seventy years from that day, the descendants of the present inhabitants of the United States would amount to One Thousand Millions!

If anyone is startled at such an assertion, this being a number greater than the present entire population of the globe, let it be remembered that it has been computed, after a careful estimate of the capabilities of America, that, with the present degree of knowledge, and without any reliance upon future discoveries in agriculture and the arts, this whole continent will sustain at least two thousand millions of inhabitants in circumstances of comfort. But the extreme nearness of this vast population to ourselves, and the consequent incalculable power which the institutions and the spirit of this present generation are to exert in molding its character and destiny, constitute the grand point of importance in every benevolent mind. Within the period when the grand-children of those now upon the stage of action shall be the actors and spectators in our stead, the population of this country will have nearly or quite reached the sum of two hundred millions. In all human experience, no community were ever placed, by their mere relative position on the banks of the stream of time, at a point of such commanding, such overwhelming influence and responsibility. The drama which successive generations have been playing on the theatre of existence, becomes a transitory, dream-like mockery, when compared with the seriousness and lasting importance of ours. Note C

> **Note C**
> We have referred to the publication by Mr. Evarts of the paper on the Moral Destiny of the United States. It is one of the most grand and eloquent productions ever issued in any shape from the American press. We well remember the electric thrill of feeling, and impression of the moral sublime produced by its first appearance as a *Report of the American Board of Commissioners for Foreign Missions*. It was written shortly before the author's death, and seems to glow not merely with the spirit of piety, but of prophecy. Its closing paragraphs are worthy of a place in the *Vade Mecum* [guide book] of every Christian Pilgrim in America.

Our population doubles once in twenty-three years. But to keep within the most probable limits, and on this side reality, we may best take the period for doubling at twenty-five years. Our population may now be safely assumed at eighteen millions. In twenty-five years from this time, in the year 1865, it will therefore be thirty-six millions. In 1888, in fifty years from this present period, it will be seventy-two millions. In seventy-five years it will amount to one hundred and forty-four millions. And in one hundred years, there will be in these United States, and by the good pleasure of God, under the same government that now blesses us, and speaking the same language which we speak, two hundred and eighty-eight millions of human beings. Going one step further in the calculation, in the space of only one hundred and twenty-five years from this day, five hundred and seventy-six millions of immortal beings will form the tremendous mass of the population of this country! The thought becomes so overwhelming, that it seems wild, chimerical, incredible. And yet, allowing the ratio between holiness and wickedness to remain even as it is, and that there be no increase in the proportion of piety in our land, even on such an unfavorable supposition, except God himself interpose, with some vast and awful judgment, the computation is sure.

Methinks now we are ready to exclaim that the welfare of such a future population of our own is an object of quite as vast importance, as the evangelization of the whole world besides. And this is most true. But it is equally true that, so far as we are concerned, the two enterprises of this country's and the world's evangelization must advance or fluctuate, stand or fall together. Our own destiny is not more indissolubly linked with the one than with the other. If we do our part for the evangelization of the world, we save ourselves; if we neglect that, we destroy ourselves. The two experiments are before us, and the one is just as completely under our control, as the other.

If the influence exerted over the thronging multitude of our posterity be such, that holiness shall grow up among us as fast as our knowledge and population, it is easy to see that the whole world's evangelization through our instrumentality is within our reach. We may soon command the moral machinery of all the globe. Not the most distant and the wildest of earth's inhabited regions, but must be moved and shaken by the impulse, whenever we touch the spring. We may take whole nations by the hand, and raise them up to civil and religious liberty, and, under God, infuse into their very framework the vital spirit of the gospel. No alliance of tyranny and superstition will be able to stand before us; by a single look we might almost frown down the strongest combinations of wickedness.

By the pure, simple, blessed, legitimate influence of united knowledge and holiness, we may exert over all nations a power more absolutely despotic, and for its spirituality, infinitely more glorious, than Rome, with all her legions, ever possessed, in the most universal extent of her empire. Let the bare existence of a truly Christian nation, with a population of five hundred millions be supposed, and the whole world's evangelization follows almost inevitably. On the other hand, if wickedness prevail, while population and knowledge increase, what imagination can picture the tumultuous frightful reign of anarchy and crime. It will be as if the infernal fiends had moved up from hell to earth, and made this the grand scene of their most gigantic operations.

9. In the light of this last topic of the increase of our population may be viewed, in the ninth place, the real importance of that great gift of God's providence to this country, the universality of a good common education. There is among us an universal diffusion of

knowledge, which is unexampled in the world. If this be continued, and the salt of divine grace be cast into our common schools, we have a security for order and happiness among ourselves, and a sure foundation of intelligent benevolent effort throughout the earth. There is no way in which we can do more for our future welfare, more to accomplish God's designs of mercy, and in the language of Scripture, raise up the foundations of many generations for the divine glory, than by devoting the most scrupulous, unremitting, religious attention to our common schools.

10. In the tenth and last place in this enumeration, the geographical position of our country must be considered as not the least among the circumstances favorable to the vast extent of our moral power. Our situation with respect to other countries and political powers, gives us security and repose. The state of all Europe is in the highest degree critical and uncertain. In the calmest times there are tremendous causes at work, volcanoes that may break forth at any moment. In a time of profound peace, I have passed, in European cities, through public squares faced with cannon, and have been pressed by the soldiery on guard, within the line of enclosure which I had transgressed. Whence was this? Was it because, in a period of excitement, or with causes existing to produce it, those squares would become the places of assemblage, and therefore must be fortified in *terrorem* [without challenge], beforehand?

Men walk, in that part of the world, over hidden, hot embers, *suppositos cineri doloso*, seemingly dead and covered with ashes, but ready at any moment to burst into a devouring flame. The elements of democracy are at work, a republican tendency and struggle is manifest, the day of retribution for ages of misrule and oppression is yet to come. Envy and discontent, the consciousness of misery and tyranny, and the desire of change, are at work in the lower ranks, without knowledge and virtue to balance and to guide. Many overturnings must take place, and perhaps an universal breaking up of the established order of things in Europe, before the preparation necessary for the coming of Christ's kingdom in power and permanence shall be found among the nations.

In comparison with ourselves, Europe is like a region at the base of a volcano. How narrowly have the nations just escaped being hurried into universal war! War is their passion and their habit, and the slightest cause may prompt it; and then the kingdoms that have heretofore been most actively engaged in the enterprises of Christian benevolence, may be thrown back in piety, and paralyzed in their spiritual energies, to an unspeakable degree. We look on, from this distant side of the world, in quiet and security. We are now, and unless the curse comes upon us for our ingratitude, and we be smitten with madness and blindness and astonishment of heart, so as to rush uncalled into the battle, we may keep ourselves to the end of time, utterly aloof from the wars and fightings that agitate and tear the bosom of the continent of Europe. We hear the din of their quarrels, the shock of their contending armies, but have no motive whatever to engage in the commotion. We may go on rapidly and silently, and peacefully in the great work to which the Lord our God hath called us, overshadowed by his wings, and supremely blessed in being made his instruments to carry the glad tidings of salvation even to the ends of the earth. As the tribe of Levi was separated from among the rest of the tribes of Israel, and consecrated to the exclusive service of Jehovah, so may this great people, while other nations are waging bitter strife, or absorbed in earthly pursuits, advance in an uninterrupted career of holy benevolence, and become God's Priesthood To A World!

Chapter 8
Designs Of God In Our Discipline, And The Blessedness Of Their Fulfillment On Our Part

Having endeavored to trace some of the circumstances of God's discipline in regard to us, and to weigh the degree of moral power over the nations which those circumstances conspire to put into our hands, it is hardly necessary to ask what are the designs of God in laying upon us such responsibilities. The responsibilities themselves indicate a mighty design, and mark out a magnificent career of duty. The blessings that constitute the foundation of our responsibilities, constitute also the revelation of God's will concerning us, and afford, at the same time, the means of fulfilling it. That the discipline of the divine providence in our case has been peculiarly grand, intense, and blessed, it would require the stupidity and blindness of an atheist to deny.

We may say with as much propriety as Israel of old, "*He hath not dealt so with any people.*" That this peculiar discipline indicates a peculiar and equally important purpose is just as manifest; and it is difficult to believe that God will suffer the moral, intellectual, and physical training of this people on so magnificent a scale, and with such vast and glorious objects to be accomplished by it, utterly to fail. Nevertheless, the voice of warning issues from the sacred word, with a solemnity deepened by the fall of the chosen people of God, after a majestic training and probation of more than a thousand years,— "*At what instant I shall speak concerning a nation and concerning a kingdom to build and to plant it, if it do evil in my sight, that it obey not my voice, then I will repent of this good wherewith I said I will benefit them.*" And the echo of this solemn declaration comes to us from the New Testament, "*Behold therefore the goodness and severity of God; on them which fell, severity, but towards thee goodness, if thou continue in his goodness, Otherwise THOU*

ALSO SHALT BE CUT OFF!"

We think there are indications which show two great lines of the Divine Providence converging. One is in the manifest general preparation going on among the nations for the accomplishment of God's great purposes, as revealed in his word; the other is in the corresponding discipline of our own country in particular. We are little more than a half century old, and yet in this time we have become a strong nation, and as a church, able, perhaps, to do more than any other in the world. The blessing of youth as a nation, at such a period as this, it is difficult to realize. Compared with the stiffness and rigidity of age in some nations, and the marks of decay in others, our spirit is as fresh and elastic, our strength as vigorous, and our mind as ductile, as if ours were indeed the glow of unperverted childhood.

We have no national habits or prejudices formed under the old order of things, and difficult to be relinquished, and there is in us a quickness and ability to embrace opportunities and conjunctures, which in the nature of things other nations cannot possess. Our religious enterprises and our benevolent societies, as well as our secular and business undertakings, have the same glow of life and activity, and almost every train of influences that could be desired is in some way or other in operation.

All this has taken place suddenly; we being like a nation born in a day, and at a time which constitutes a great crisis, a radiating point, a magnetic pole, as it were, in the world's history. There is a universal movement in society, a new arrangement of its elements, an increase of its inventions and discoveries, the casting up of a grand highway of the Gospel among the nations. There is a cluster of events and thoughts, in the present aspect of things, of great power and significance. It is but three or four centuries since the very first discovery of this continent by Columbus. In connection with that world-awakening event, and as if on purpose to secure it from being turned into the service of the Man of Sin, then ascendant and triumphant through the nations, came the great religious irradiation, the Reformation through the instrumentality of Luther, the discovery of a new world of piety and intellect for men's souls to dwell in.

About the same period, and as if on purpose to fulfill the designs of God in those events, the invention of printing rose into useful and almost universal application. Immediately upon these things, almost as suddenly as report succeeds report in the earthquakes that shake the physical world, followed the preparation and planting of a church of Christ and a Protestant nation growing out of it in this country; a church and a nation whose increase and results are watched with an intense interest, in comparison with which the whole continent besides, from north to south, scarcely attracts attention. Meanwhile, knowledge is everywhere increasing, steamships traverse the ocean, the barriers material and moral, between the nations, are breaking down, and old systems, religious and political, are fast giving way.

Bringing thus into one view some of the most grand and prominent events in the world's recent history, and remembering that at this moment our own population has reached a census, from which it is to rise with a suddenness that is almost startling, to the highest amount admissible in the nature of things upon this continent, we cannot but feel that we are upon the very eve of a development of great grandeur and importance.

The lines of prophecy are converging, and the trains of God's providence are growing nearer and more crowded, as if deepening to a great center, and indicating some mighty consummation, just as the near approach to a vast metropolis is indicated by the multiplied avenues, the augmented crowds, and the increasing grandeur of the buildings. With every division and variety of its processes concentering [sic] to one sublime purpose, the plan of God moves forward to its completion. Empires and armies, wars, whirlwinds, and pestilences, evil men and devils, good institutions and bad ones, commotions and revolutions, all prepare his way. He goes on overturning, and overturning, and overturning, and when about to revive his work, and in wrath remember mercy, sometimes the signs among the nations are more full of commotion and terribleness than ever.

There is certainly no presumption in the supposition that God has created, is educating, and will sustain a peculiar people to accomplish his great purposes at such a crisis. Whether there be any presumption in the supposition that we ourselves are marked and destined for so great and glorious an instrumentality, depends much upon our own manifestation of character thus far, beneath the divine discipline, and upon the right study and interpretations of the divine providence. We cannot but hope, looking at the present state of the globe, and at the peculiarities of our own national and ecclesiastical history, that God is preparing the political and social relations of the world for the philanthropic movements of a nation and a church so constituted and disciplined.

The divine providence has as marked and definite a meaning in regard to nations as to individuals, and sometimes even more manifest. In this view, there is, if I may so speak, the commencement of a new phase of prophecy, and the grandeur of the scriptures, in their national proclamations, will arrest every mind. A change passes over the prophetic canvass; it is filled with grand and august figures. God is coming to use nations like individuals, for the fulfillment of his purposes. His long rejected people, the Jews, begin to appear in the picture, and those two great lines of prophecy, running consentaneously upon them and other nations, seem ready to unite in that point of glory indicated by the great apostle to the Gentiles, when the coming in of the fullness of the Gentiles and the salvation of the Jews together, as mutual cause and effect, shall fill the world with righteousness, and hasten the scheme of redemption to its completion.

Let us look, for a moment, at the blessedness of the fulfillment, on our part, of the great designs of the divine providence, so marked and manifest in regard to us. On the supposition, that, as a people, we fulfill our personal duties to God, and grow in holiness in proportion as we grow in power, the only supposition on which the church ought to act; the supposition, indeed, which the church is bound to realize; the picture that unfolds before the mind of the Christian, is such an one as might employ the pencil of Isaiah. We may realize, indeed, the brightest visions of holiness, mercy, and happiness, contained in the scriptural delineations of the reign of the Prince of peace. As individual Christians, we may sit each under his own vine and fig tree, and devoutly study our Bibles and grow in grace beneath the influences of the sanctuary, and no war shall desolate our habitation, or grieve away the Spirit of the Lord. We may walk about Zion, and tell the towers thereof, and glory in her increasing strength, and mark well her bulwarks, and consider her palaces, and meet together to pray and consult for the advancement of the cause and kingdom of our Savior, and none shall molest us or make us afraid.

As a nation of Christians, we may be a crown of glory in the hand of the Lord, and a royal diadem in the hand of our God. We may increase in spiritual wisdom and humility, and universal devotedness to God, till holiness shall be written even on the bells of our horses; till our officers become peace, our exactors [sic] righteousness, and every place religion. We may cover our land with goodly temples rising to the peaceful worship of Jehovah, till from every elevation the eye may rest upon their consecrated spires. We may multiply societies of benevolence till misery shall scarcely be known, and allurements to reformation, till hardly a prison shall rear its black walls to the sight. No slave shall then breathe in our air, or tremble, in this land of freedom, beneath the rod of a taskmaster. Every yoke shall be broken, every evil statute cancelled, and the oppressed shall go free. Violence shall no more be heard in our land, wasting nor destruction in our borders; we may call our walls salvation, and our gates praise. We may build up the schools of the prophets, and send the Bible to every family, and a faithful, affectionate pastor to every hamlet, till the days of our mourning shall be ended, and the cry of the spiritually destitute no more heard among us till indeed it shall be said of us, *"Thy people are all righteous."*

Then no ordinance in our country's statute book shall legalize the national violation of the Sabbath, and no rude noise of secular business intrude upon its heavenly repose. Here I cannot forbear a quotation from the sublime language of that eloquent production of the former Secretary of the American Board, to which I have already referred. Speaking of the time *"when all the happy millions of this continent shall live together as brethren, adoring their Creator and Redeemer,"* *"Then,"* said Mr. Evarts, *"will be a day of glory, such as the world has never yet witnessed. As the sun rises on a Sabbath morning, and travels westward from Newfoundland to the Oregon, he will behold the countless millions assembling, as if by a common impulse, in the temples with which every valley, mountain, and plain will be adorned. The morning psalm and evening anthem will commence with the multitudes on the Atlantic coast, be sustained by the loud chorus of ten thousand times ten thousand in the Valley of the Mississippi, and prolonged by the thousands of thousands on the shores of the Pacific. Throughout this wide expanse, not a dissonant voice will be heard. If, unhappily, there should be here and there an individual whose heart is not in unison with this divine employment he will choose to be silent. Then the tabernacle of God will be with men. Then will it be seen and known to the universe, what the religion of the Bible can do even on this side the grave, for a penitent, restored, and rejoicing world."*

But this is not all; it is the spirit of MISSIONS which constitutes the spirit and power even of a vital home religion. Happy in the care of Him, who visits and redeems his people, blest with civil and religious freedom, and enjoying all the privileges of the sanctuary ourselves, we may carry forth these blessings to the darkest and most sorrowful corner of the earth. We may enlarge and strengthen our missionary societies, till their power is felt through the habitable world, till their ministers of mercy go forth to tell the farthest and saddest outcasts of Israel that Christ died to redeem them. With no foreign armaments to support, and no exhausting wars to drain us of our wealth, we may pour incalculable riches into the Lord's treasury for the heathen.

We may in literal truth cause the outgoings of the morning and of the evening to rejoice at the footsteps of our benevolence. We may become the main instrument, in the hands of Jehovah, of accomplishing the day and the state of universal millennial glory. In the sweet language of Isaiah, whenever he speaks of such a period, the wilderness and the solitary place shall be glad for us, and the desert shall rejoice and blossom as the rose. We may apply to ourselves the blessed predictions of the prophet, in all their fullness and sublimity.

What we may do is but the index of what we ought. What God, in his providence, has given us the ability and the opportunity to accomplish, becomes our duty to perform. For it is as true of nations as of individuals, that To Him That KNOWETH TO DO GOOD, AND DOETH IT NOT, TO HIM IT IS SIN.

Chapter 9
Interest And Grandeur Of The Divine Experiment With Us As A People, Conditions Of Success, Causes At Work To Disturb And Thwart It

We cannot conceal from ourselves, nor would we wish to do it, that the responsibilities of every kind resting upon this country are mightier than those which belong to any other nation in the world. Especially is this the case with the religious responsibilities of a Christian church which God has so remarkably blessed. If we redeem them, it will be glorious for us and glorious for the world. It is good for us, on this mount of vision, commanding on all sides an immense moral view, to call to mind our multiplied responsibilities, and see what sublime motives animate us onward. We stand upon a lofty and imposing situation. We are compassed about by a great cloud of witnesses, being made a spectacle, not only to the world, but to an innumerable company of angels and the spirits of the just made perfect. It may be no dream of the imagination, but an undoubted reality, that higher orders of intelligences are watching our movements with intense interest, and that Paul, and Peter, and John, and all the beloved apostles of our Savior, and all who have since trod in their footsteps, and through toil and pain and death inherited the promises, are looking down upon us, and waiting, I had almost said with painful anxiety, the result of this mighty experiment. It seems as if Heaven had placed our country in this situation to try us; to see whether we would faithfully use the incalculable power in our hands for speeding forward the world's regeneration, and if not, how many accumulated blessings we could waste and reject.

In contemplating the picture of our happiness in a course of national piety, and in making such an enumeration of our national talents for a wide moral influence, we are not to forget that it is only through a probation of severe and holy discipline, that we can hope to arrive at the attainment of such glory. Nor must we for a moment let the remembrance pass from our minds, that it is *"not by might, nor by power, But By My Spirit, Saith The Lord Of Hosts,"* that the great work is to be accomplished. We may have had the noblest and most pious ancestry on earth; we may possess the freest institutions, the strongest physical power, the most inexhaustible wealth, the highest foreign influence and reputation ; we may enjoy the most universal diffusion of knowledge; and what is more than all, the Spirit of God may be poured out upon us for a time in accumulated revivals of religion; and yet we may turn every one of our vast capabilities to ruin, except God keep us humble, and preserve in us a spirit of deep contrition and dependence on him.

Besides, there is another and a widely different view of our whole subject. There is a gloomier prospect in the probabilities of our country's future destiny. There is at least one dark spot in our moral and political horizon. Yet we cannot suffer ourselves to believe that God will permit, with the growth of our nation in [population] and power, the continuance of the enormous evil of Slavery, the indulgence of that great sin, which would inevitably prove the destruction of all our hopes of usefulness and glory. If he should do this, and give us over, like his ancient people, to our own heart's lusts then we should indeed become a signal and terrible example of God's holy indignation. Then, in the prophetic language of Milton, and with allusion to our past extraordinary history, *"as if God were weary of protecting us, we shall be seen to have passed through the fire, that we might perish in, the smoke."* For we cannot ourselves remain free, and yet persist in imposing bondage on others. *"And it usually happens,"* (that great writer profoundly remarks in his Second Defense of the People of England,) *"by the appointment, and as it were retributive justice of the Deity, that that people which cannot govern themselves, and moderate their passions, but voluntarily crouch under the slavery of their lusts, should be delivered up to the sway of those whom they abhor, and made to submit to an involuntary servitude."* But if after all our lofty privileges and excitements to glory, we do deny God, and turn from following his pleasure, to follow our own depravity, and fill up the measure of our iniquities, then our fall and punishment must be a second Jewish tragedy on a wider and more awful scale, and all the curses written in the book of the law cannot but descend upon us. *"And it shall come to pass that the generation to come, that shall rise up after us, and the stranger that shall come from a far land, shall say, when they shall see the plagues of this land, and the sicknesses which the Lord hath laid upon it, and that the whole land is brimstone and salt, and burning, that it is not sown, nor beareth, nor any grass groweth therein, like the overthrow of Sodom and Gomorrah, Admah and Zeboim, which the Lord overthrew in his anger and in his wrath;— even all nations shall say, Wherefore hath the Lord done thus unto this land? What meaneth the heat of this great anger?"*

Perhaps we are in danger of indulging a sort of indolent pleasure in the expectation that the millennium is soon to open on the world, without reflecting how great must be the increase of personal piety for along previous period, how deep, severe, and self-denying must be the probationary discipline of the church, and how little we know what unexpected means God may take to signalize the glorious scheme of redemption, or what may be the duration or the nature of the scene that is yet to come of his moral administration on this globe. For aught we know, the passions of mankind may yet again be let loose to rage and devastate through a long and dreary duration of moral gloom; the fountains of the great deep may be broken up, and a deluge of wickedness heave its vast surges over the earth, till scarce a vestige of the great moral landmarks even of Christianity itself can be discovered. This may take place after a universal diffusion of every kind of knowledge, the speculative knowledge even of the Scriptures not excepted, that it may be shown on a scale as broad as the earth, that the highest and most widely diffused intellectual refinement without regeneration will be no sort of barrier to the violence of human depravity, but on the contrary, by increasing its ingenuity, augment tenfold its dire and untamable fury.

God may offer the precious gift of the Gospel to every nation under heaven, and it may be in turn proudly and awfully rejected by them all; and after leaving it to be demonstrated by the universal wickedness of men that of all modern ages and nations, with all their boasted superiority and improvements, there is not one but will outdo in depravity that ancient people, so long an astonishment and a byword, he may take the cup of trembling from them, and make every Christian people drink it to the dregs. He may leave their own infuriated wickedness to sweep from all Christendom the light of holy truth, and then, when the Bible is a proscribed book, to be read only by stealth, and when earth seems about to become the empire of Satan, he may appear in his glory, and build up Jerusalem, and bring back from their dispersion his ancient covenant people, and use them as the willing, grateful instruments in carrying the religion of that Savior whom their fathers crucified, forth from the scene of his sufferings into every quarter of the globe.

Though this be all hypothetical and visionary, yet we do not know that there is any thing in the record of prophecy to conflict with the supposition or the possibility of such an additional scene in the great instructive drama, which God is permitting to be played in this world, and which he will suffer to be played out without interruption. At any rate, however far the designs of God's providence may seem manifested and in process of execution in regard to ourselves, and however important the instrumentality of a nation and a church so trained and disciplined might appear in the midst of a world so depraved and degraded, it becomes us to remember that as God out of the stones in the streets of Jerusalem could have raised up children unto Abraham, so he can now just as easily accomplish his purposes and his prophecies without our aid.

Chapter 10
Lessons Of Individual Responsibility And Duty, A High Standard Of Piety, A Holy Education, The Right Use Of Property, The Right Use Of Prayer, Conclusion

In the mirror of this great subject we behold reflected the solemnity and responsibility of our position as individual Christians. It teaches the necessity of an immediate elevation of our individual standard of piety.

The resolution of the mighty problem as to the world's evangelization by us, rests more entirely on the holiness of individual Christians than any of us can possibly conceive. Wherever there is an eminently holy saint in our country, there is one of the pillars of our greatness. When such an individual dies, if there be none to take his place, the shock sustained in his departure is irretrievable. Looking back upon the American Church in all her past history, we shall find, in every period, that her advancing strength has resulted from the eminent piety of a few distinguished Christians. Blot out, if it could be done, the name and memory of Brainard and Edwards, and draw off from our system by a mighty moral exhaustion the influence which their characters have exerted in building up our country's church, and we should blot out some of the fairest of her Christian graces; we should draw away the very life-blood in her veins. Let the same be done with a few other holy individuals, and though diminished as to numbers, but little in every ten thousand of our ranks, we should be left faint, exhausted, prostrate in the dust, and able to prosecute hardly the smallest of our present widely-extended enterprises.

Great numbers do but encumber our moral vigor, unless holiness increases in a greater ratio. Doubtless, the piety of many is so low, that the holy minority could do better without them. It would be better to proclaim, as when God sent Gideon against the Midianites, *"whoever is fearful and afraid, let him return and depart early;"* and if then only the efficient part were chosen out, there would hardly remain, as on that occasion, three hundred out of every thirty-two thousand.

We do not sufficiently consider, that to sustain great operations abroad, we must have a deeper piety at home. The self-denial of our missionaries, must be sustained by the self-denial of the Church; nor ought we to be willing to live at ease in America, and deny ourselves only by proxy in Africa or Asia. Moreover, the power and success of our missionaries among the heathen will depend upon the power in prayer and holy living possessed by the churches that sustain them. But a small portion of our work is done, even when we have provided the men, and sent them abroad with the gospel of life in their hands ; they are still connected with us, and greatly dependent on our piety:

"They drag at each remove a lengthening chain,"

and if we do not communicate an electric, life-giving impulse, it will prove a perpetual clog. They are the clouds that take the water of life from this continent, and wafted by the breath of prayer, sail away to pour it down on the thirsty land of the heathen. If the fountains here be shallow, it can fall there only in scanty and inconstant showers.

It is to be feared that we are daily and hourly departing wider and wider from the searching, self-examining, closet piety of our fathers, and becoming more and more exclusively external in our efforts. We are living on the patrimony that has descended to us, without continuing to increase it by the same labor, with which it was acquired. It may be all gone before we are aware; and if we do not keep up the fires beneath, our whole machinery will suddenly stop.

It is by no means a matter of course, that the next generation of Christians will be more devoted, more holy, and self-denying than we. The next generation will be molded by the spirit of our piety, and if they should grow up in our external and undevout habits, there would be even less of spirituality in them than in us. The natural course of things, owing to the powerful tendency of the heart to depart from God, is downwards; declension, not advancement; a truth which is not more perfectly displayed in the history of the Hebrews, than in that of the whole Gentile Church; and the grand lesson we are to derive from it, is the necessity of a high standard of individual piety. Even in the midst of external prosperity, we must enter into our closets, and shut the door, and pray to our Father in secret. What we admit speculatively, we must feel and acknowledge practically, that the missionary work, in all its departments, from the foundation in Christendom to the completion amidst heathenism, is a purely spiritual work, and demands spiritual instruments. It demands, not grand and powerful societies merely, but self-denial, deadness to the world, spiritual habits, clear views of eternity, knowledge of the Bible, consciousness of the value of the soul, an affecting sense of the insignificance of earthly things, deep love to Christ, strong and panting desires after the glory of God. It demands that the Church, like the soul, should rise out of the vanities of time into the riches of eternity, and take hold on God by faith, with a moral courage and an endurance of fatigue, of which we have little conception. If the Church will not learn this in sunshine, perhaps God will teach it in persecution, for the work of missions cannot go forward without deep piety. It would be a falsification of the whole spirit and tenor of the Gospel, if it were found that men or Churches can engage in the labors of Christianity, and obtain its glorious rewards, without self-denial, deadness to the world, spirituality of heart and life, incessant prayer; without partaking somewhat in the trials as well as the enjoyments of the apostolic Christians; without the elements inaction of the same enduring faith and dauntless moral courage, which in them burned so brightly. It is one of the signets of the Christian Religion, which we may well believe God will never suffer to be entirely blotted out, that *through much tribulation we must enter into the kingdom of Heaven.*

It is in the light of such a survey as we have taken of the divine discipline towards us, and especially of our rapidly advancing population, that I love to view our individual responsibilities and duties. It gives to every movement of benevolence and piety, especially if connected with the training of the rising generation, an indescribable dignity and importance. The business of preparing the materials for the fulfillment of the divine purposes, the business of molding the minds and hearts of those whose character and conduct are to decide this grand experiment, places those engaged in it at the very springs of our country's future greatness; it makes them the guardians of the vast hopes which the gracious indications of God's providence lead us to form for ourselves and for the world.

Never before, in the history of the world, have great results been brought so near to their apparently trifling causes. If an angelic visitant to our globe, or a being from another planet were in the midst of us, desiring to be made acquainted with the sources of our future destiny, I would take him to some of the most unostentatious and unnoticed spheres of industry and piety; he should visit an unpretending common school, a Sabbath school, a tract-distributor's prayer-meeting. Viewed in their results, and looking a few years onward, these humble spheres of duty become the centers of a mighty influence and responsibility.

The teacher of a common school in this country, bringing before his mind the period which he can almost touch and mingle in himself, when the pupils whose moral and intellectual frame he is molding, shall stand amidst seventy millions more in the strife of existence, to be the parents of those with whom there shall stand up four hundred millions, cannot but feel that there is a solemn responsibility as well as a blessed privilege connected with his duties. The Sabbath school teacher, who pursues his sacred round of duty faithfully, in love and prayer, looking to the nearness and incalculable glory of its results, may wonder at the grace of God in permitting him to occupy a post of so much importance and blessedness. The mother, who seeks, in humble dependence on the grace of Christ, to find the reflection of his blessed image in the opening mind even of her infant offspring, and to train her beloved children from their earliest hours, into habits of obedience and piety, is doing a work for the happiness of her race, the salvation of the world, and the glory of the Redeemer, which angels might envy for its simplicity, its beauty, and its grandeur. And in every sphere of influence that can be mentioned, we are made to feel the mingled blessedness and responsibility of occupying a place in the world at such a crisis;— a period when every movement tells so directly in great results, both for time and eternity.

The consideration of this subject, teaches us the right use of property, and the great value of it, when devoted, at such a crisis, to God. It is rarely, if ever, in the world's history, that an opportunity has been offered to the rich, of engaging, by their wealth alone, in movements of such intense glory. The Divine Being ordinarily avoids even the appearance of magnifying the instrumentality of wealth in human estimation. He calls us to stand beside his treasury, and as our eye scans the persons of the comers, and the costliness of their offerings, he tells us that this poor, unnoticed widow, whose loving heart consecrated in two mites her whole living, hath cast in more than they all. So it is in every age; and every widow's mite, as well as the precious incense of her prayers, is needed, and at a time like this, goes immediately to a result of practical utility, of incalculable importance.

Nevertheless, to those Christians whom God has permitted to amass wealth, a post of usefulness is now offered, in the support of theological and missionary institutions languishing by pecuniary pressure, which, considered in the magnitude and nobleness of its results, is truly sublime, and which, if they beheld it with the eye of faith, they would exult, like the angels of God, with gratitude and praise to occupy. And the Churches of Christ in this country are called upon to give a steadiness to the Missionary Enterprise by the steadfast abundance of their offerings, and not to leave the sacred cause to fluctuate, and the hearts of those engaged in it to sink and die within them, in the perpetual prospect of poverty and disaster. Is it possible that in the midst of all our responsibilities and opportunities of glory, we can consent to leave our benevolent societies to languish and die from pecuniary starvation, and that, too, at a period which is the very harvest time of the world? God forbid that we should be guilty of so dishonorable a betrayal of the trust committed to our care!

Above all, we are taught by this great subject, the necessity of fervent prayer. It is nothing but God's grace that can enable us to redeem the responsibilities that rest upon us ; nothing but his Holy Spirit poured out in revivals of religion that can save us from absolute and most tremendous destruction. That Christian therefore, who is doing most for the promotion of a revival of religion in his own church, and that church which is laboring most fervently for a revival in its own village or city, is doing most, and most directly, for the conversion of the world. O! in the light of our advancing population, who can estimate the importance of one revival of piety! And here the poorest, most unlettered Christian may bear a part, and a great part, in the advancement of the Redeemer's kingdom. This surely is our grand field of labor, and the consummation of predicted glory waits for the Church of Christ to enter upon it.

Let it be remembered that every Christian in this country possesses as much power to intercede for the millions of China as he does for the children of his own household or the families in his own neighborhood. Blessed is he who realizes the privilege of prayer and uses it accordingly. The period will arrive when, for every half hour given to the business of intercessory communion with God, the Christian will wish he had given days, and for every little sacrifice made in this cause he will wish he had made a thousand. The time will come, when the memory of the shortest interval so spent, of the smallest sacrifice so made, will be a possession of glory to the soul, which he would not part with for the riches of the material universe!

Blessing, And Honor, And Glory, And Power, Be Unto Him That Sitteth Upon The Throne, And Unto The Lamb For EVER AND EVER!

> Men well governed should seek after no other liberty, for there can be no greater liberty than a good government. --Sir Walter Raleigh.

> The distinguishing part of our constitution is its liberty. But the only liberty I mean, is a liberty connected with order; a liberty that not only exists along with order and virtue, but which cannot exist at all without them. --Burke.

www.ingramcontent.com/pod-product-compliance
Lightning Source LLC
Chambersburg PA
CBHW071513040426
42444CB00008B/1621